ACKNOW

CW01501576

There have literally bee⌐ throughout my life contr⌐ experiences and skills with me. So I thank you ....

The most important and influential people though are first, my Heavenly Father who has given me all and had a hand in my life from day one;

Then my husband who has always stepped back to let me do my thing and watched me fly, coming along for the ride no matter how inconvenient or annoying. He too has brought me so much love and joy;

Then there's my children who have been a part of my journey learning about myself as far as developing patience, endurance and most of all, for filling my heart swell with love and joy;

My parents who against all odds and without a manual actually managed to raise someone who isn't all together nuts, who did the best they could to teach me to survive and thrive. My dad for sharing his artistic talents with me, my mum for her amazing make do and mend, homemaking, frugal skills that have been the biggest influence in giving me skills to ensure my family never went hungry, cold or neglected;

I'd also like to acknowledge my best friend Chris, who encourages and supports me in everything I do and shares so many of my hobbies and passions as far as style, crafts and nature go.

Everything I do and am is a culmination of generations of people, their influence and experiences which have all come together to help me recognize where I am in the evolution of Blue Garden Cottage.

Escaping the Dole to Blue Garden Cottage

SINDY WAKEHAM

DEDICATION

I dedicate this book to my hubby who tries to make sure I have every opportunity to write by removing interruptions, also to my bestie who encourages and guides me daily. Most importantly I dedicate this book to my Heavenly Father in gratitude for the opportunity and yearning to share, and for his hand in my meeting all the people and learning from many who all contributed to me being able to do this.

SINDY WAKEHAM

CONTENTS

SINDY WAKEHAM

1
FOR STARTERS

Where to begin? Blue Garden Cottage is what I named my YouTube channel. The channel is where I share a few of the things I do as part of my husband's and my self-reliance and freedom from social welfare journey. Particularly around our garden and the intention of growing our own throughout the year and in all seasons, preserving in a not so complicated way, food storage, homemaking, crafting and my endeavours to write and create digital products to sell. With TV reruns like The Good Life, reality programmes following Brits moving abroad and living off grid and off the land being our inspiration during the early years of our marriage, we set about living our lives in a way that would ultimately lead to that goal becoming reality. Don't worry if that romantic ideal makes you feel sick. It hasn't quite worked out the way we planned.

Things never really work out exactly to plan. Each new challenge appears to take us further away from the ultimate goal. I am determined that whatever life throws at us and whatever situation we find ourselves in, I'm going to forge it into that dream, one way or another.

That early inspiration of living off the land and in the countryside was a strong desire I felt was a deep part of me and what my hubby and I, were always meant to be and do. Well, me. I'm fortunate enough to have a hubby that stands back and watches me spread my wings and soar in whatever direction I choose and supports me by coming along and helping me achieve my goals even if it scares or stresses him. He's a good'un.

Some of the events or situations leading us away from the rural dream were physical illness and becoming dependent on the welfare system. Being raised in a culture where if you don't work you don't survive and work being a part of our natures, suddenly having to depend on social welfare we were in that world of negative connotations, narratives and attitudes from both ourselves and society in general. At that time there was a stigma and label attached to those social welfare, that for folk like us, was a trauma. There still is today but not so much as or in the same way as in the past.

How did we get from there to here? That's what I'm going to be sharing with you. I'll be venting just a bit, not too much. I'm sharing with you a few of our budgeting, planning and frugal tools and tactics that have been helpful this far. There will be lots of frilly trips down memory lane as I delve into the core roots of why I feel such a connection with my goals. I'm not going to apologize for that. It's how I discovered my big WHY. The big WHY led to a big AWAKENING and realisation completely changing everything, the direction we were going and what has led to Blue Garden Cottage from that point.

My hope is that by sharing just some of those experiences, memories and tools, someone somewhere, hopefully YOU, will be moved forward in their/your own dreams, desires and ambitions. Hopefully if you are stuck in the system who really want to get out of it, this may give you ideas you might not have considered...and just maybe I can spread some smiles. If you didn't already know, smiles are as contagious as a cold.

So what qualifies me to share? If we're talking paper qualifications, I have one Diploma in holistic therapy, a PDC (Permaculture Design Certificate), and a few other certificates of study in subjects from bookkeeping and food hygiene to Edible Landscaping.

None of those qualify me as much as the experiences of my own life and the examples of others around me. Those experiences and examples all work together giving me the tools needed to navigate a mortal journey and make the most of it including the skill to make my dreams a reality in spite of opposition.

Oh, and there are also innumerable hours of study at 'The University of YouTube'. That's a joke hubby and I share about the amount of time we spend studying and implementing the things learned on YouTube. Surely it adds up to a university qualification of some sort by now (I wish I could put a laughing emoji right here). Oh, and since we first used that term over 15 years ago, it's become a buzz word on YouTube, just saying.

Anyway, I'm not trying to teach, impress or instruct anyone. I AM simply sharing and chatting with you about some of the memories and foundations of my life combining to help hubby and I get that 'Good Life' we've been dreaming about.

There's a massive 'You've Been Tangoed' moment (just type; Advert 1: Tango-Orange Man on YouTube and you'll know what I mean). Then there's some 'getting down to making things happen' tactics.

By the way,please don't go expecting a literary work of genius or even perfect grammar and form. I'm writing conversationally and include all sorts of flowery words which in the literary industry are called 'dirty words'. There WILL be unnecessary words (filter words) and phrases plus a few more. The pros say it gives your work an amateur or novice appearance and isn't very professional. I really don't care and couldn't be bothered with that kind of pretence.

I'm not **trying** to be professional nor impress an Editor. I'm pouring out my heart and I'm less concerned with grammatical correctness. However, I will at least do the formatting and spell checks and try to keep it a short book. It's not a novel after all.

You've probably guessed by now that I'm self-publishing too. The only way to go in today's world with mainstream publishers being so finicky.

I'm writing according to my own rules and WILL continue self-publishing to keep that freedom. That's also because I'm practicing what I preach about frugality... and I'm temporarily skint! I'd appreciate your support in sharing with your contacts if you find any value in this book.

2
DREAMS AND LIGHTBULB MOMENTS

You know, when I started writing this chapter, I was taking stock of 2020 and all the consequences surrounding it. I was running out all the things happening on the side attached to it. By the time I had listed all my thoughts about the political excuses and fingers pointed at all the many events blamed for economic troubles along the years since 2008 globally, nationally and personally, I just had to rewrite the whole lot!

Seriously! 2020 Began with so much excitement, clarity and direction in our home. Projects were begun and plans made and implemented. As per usual with New Year's, everything was changing all over the place. The year also came like a slap in the face! I know I don't have to go into detail. I'll spare you.

What I'm about to say is only to set a context around the main reason for the chapter heading. The last thing I or anyone else for that matter would want is to have the whole chapter crammed with doom and gloom. Well maybe some folks like a bit of drama but I think we have all had enough of that, thank you very much!

We've faced financial troubles around the world before recent events struck and yes, it has been forecast to get worse with the likes of another 'Great Depression'. Not even going to mention environmental issues and the not so behind closed doors global domination agendas of certain organizations. Wink, wink, nudge, nudge.

Even so, daily life continues and we duck and dive in all sorts of directions to make ends meet and get on with it while the powers that be do their ridiculous thing...things.

We can't go around with blinkers on pretending 'it's all a hoax'. It does affect our daily lives of course. My concern is that it takes a huge amount of effort and becomes all time consuming to the point that we feel we are spending every last ounce of energy just to survive. How long can we keep doing that? If we hear the gloom repeatedly and for long enough it becomes the norm and we no longer take any notice of it.

There comes a point where belts CAN'T be tightened any further, pennies are worthless so can't be stretched; downsizing is as downsized as possible and...

You get my point, I'm sure. There's still uncertainty to say the least and probably will be for a long time. As the old idiom goes; 'it could always be worse'.

I'm sure there'll be people around the world who would hear that and want to slap me for it because it may already be much worse for them. I'm coming from a right here and right now in my own life point. For our family it certainly COULD have been and could get worse. It's not putting on blinkers. It IS survival.

It is what it is...a shambles and folks have to get by as best we can with the not so normal running of our lives. The past decade has set a trend of negative and poverty or scarcity mindset habits. I aim to change that in at least my own life and hopefully in the minds of those reading this book.

What do YOU do when you hit that wall where there just isn't any getting around or over it? Of course you won't easily be able to see a way around or over it. There's a ruddy great wall right up close! Obviously you're going to have to take a few steps back, right?

Along with all those dark stormy clouds and solid brick walls come the silver linings, rainbows of hope and opportunities to remember and remind ourselves just how blessed we really are. Too cliché? Just hold your horses.

Hitting a brick wall and getting to a point where there just aren't any options left except one is not always a bad thing. Sometimes we have to hit that point of only one way to change it; time to stop, reset and make a new plan. 2020 was the beginning of a global reset and it forced millions to push their own reset buttons. For some it was chosen rather than forced on them.

I'm convinced there's another one coming but I'll keep that theory to myself. It was and still is amazing to me the amount of gardening that became a necessity rather than the trend since 2020. Never before have I seen the seed stands and gardening supplies run out so fast. It was 'Dig for Victory' again. It's the stuff of epic movies, or history made or repeating itself for sure.

The ridiculous panic buying and shortages were a driving force where that was concerned but in the midst of all that chaos and fear, heartache and trauma, people were not just demonstrating the worst in human behaviour but also the best. There was community again even in lockdowns and people didn't let even those restrictions get in the way of their health, finding creative ways to stay fit and healthy, get closer to family, find alternative ways of earning money and loads more to celebrate. I know and recognise that some families had the most traumatic time anyone could imagine. My heart ached for them.

Truly a 'new normal' was formed for many.

Does it mean those people were just fortunate no to have to struggle like they never actually hit that brick wall? Maybe for a few but everyone else did hit that wall. It was Huge! So I suppose you get my drift...A wall is an opportunity for a reset. And it may just turn out to be the start of something better than you ever would have done had you not got a bit bruised hitting that obstacle.

Who knows what will be by the time it all passes and by the time you get this book. The only thing we do all know is nothing is the same and surely we CAN'T go back to the way we lived before. Generally and environmentally speaking, we definitely can't go back to old ways of extraction, consumerism, speculation and everything else. It's more of what we had and it contributed in some way to the problems in the first place. Both environmentally and socially we'll be back in crisis much quicker than before if we drag our feet and don't change.

Change isn't always a bad thing. I was chuffed to see more of Permaculture and its many branches like no-dig, forest gardening and food forests as well as alternative farming practices being the new topics in general media. What an opportunity we have now to put things in place so that if ever it hits the fan again, we can handle it a lot better. That's what we'd hope for, right? We do still need manufacturing and resources but have an opportunity to do it in a more positive and regenerative way moving forward. It takes getting more creative.

With economics and politics still being the stupid crazy that it is, we're all still in survival mode. Or are we? That's a scarcity mindset statement that isn't helping.

Moving forward includes technology and therewith yes, still some extraction but making things reparable and recyclable as the rule until extraction is obsolete. We can use APPROPRIATE technology fit for a cleaner, greener and more people and planet friendly future world. There will never be a utopia and in fact that's not entirely a good idea because in some dark recesses of the idea, hides the possibility of freedom to choose being lost. That's a topic for another time.

If I haven't already lost you by now on my tangent, you probably already have it all worked out and are thriving in YOUR 'new normal'. Because you are still here reading, I thank you. You must be made of tough stuff. You're my hero.

The chapter heading was about dreams and Lightbulb moments. We've already covered the Lightbulb moments in the reset idea. Personally, I've had more than one reset moment since then. Those moments of illumination can only come when you hit figurative walls and you are forced to find a way over or around it. So I'm not thinking of walls as a negative thing but rather an opportunity thing. I'm working on an abundance mindset shift.

So what about the DREAMS point? There've been questions on my mind since the global reset. What about you? Did you have dreams and ambitions pre-2020 and if so, do you still have them? Have your priorities and dreams changed and do they even matter anymore? Have your ideas changed? What if that reset or different resets for you personally since then have brought about new or different opportunities to still have your dreams but now you can change it up and make it happen in a totally different way?

What if that global 'reset button' brought a new way of looking at life let alone your dreams? It's had that effect for millions around the world. It was for me.

I had my own reset button triggered the year before a global button was pushed. In our home, we are familiar with change and it's the one constant thing. We still maintain our home, garden and need to provide help to the less self-reliant (out of necessity) family members. That's going to be changing. We still have our dream and ambition for self-reliance and a version of self-sufficiency but it's now more in line with the way we really want to go.

I've heard it said that a change is as good as a break. Change and a break is exactly what I got in the summer of 2019. There was a chance to stop, take stock, accept what is, renew goals and plan. Breaks and change are what bring action and realization. Isn't everything we use and know, begun with a dream conceived in moments of rest and reflection or out of need to adapt to change?

So what about those dreams? Do you still have a dream? That question brings back memories. A chorus actually...'you've got to have a dream. If you don't have a dream, how're you going to have a dream come true?' That's 'Happy Talk' from the 1958 movie South Pacific. Such a happy tune! It was long before my time but in primary school (1970's) every year, each year group had to prepare and deliver a concert. Our year chose that song as part of our performance,fond memories. And THAT IS my point, memories.

I want to take you on a trip down memory lane but before I do, I want to repeat my question...Do you still have a dream?

My next question is do you still have obstacles and brick walls getting in the way of achieving goals, ambitions and realizing dreams?

The problem is that being mortal; trials and obstacles are a part of mortal life. It would help if they didn't come one after another in quick succession or even before the previous one passes...nor a whole bunch at once. In our own lives, hubby and I have both (like most people) had trials, traumas and accidents for most of our lives and even after we got married, life did and still throws us those sometimes mountainous trials. At times I think that if we had to tell or write about it, we'd be called either liars or very creative in fiction.

Don't worry; I'm not going to bore you with ALL the details. Truly, I'm surprised you've made it this far! My point is that sometimes it seems there's a real being or entity shadowing our lives who just loves wrecking our goals and dreams. It feels that way to me. In my mind's eye and in my vivid imagination, the creature looks like a hydra. You know? Like the one in the movie Willow (That's giving away my age). The mythological monster growing another two heads for each one chopped off. You get rid of or solve obstacles and even more pop up in its place!

Stick with me. I promise it's not all gloom. This'll all be dripping with sweetness soon. So I hope you've got a sweet tooth. Ok, I'll water it down a bit…maybe.

Going back to memories, we all face a choice when the bad days knock the wind out of us. How we respond or react to them makes the difference between breakdown and moving forward. We can sacrifice the now for constantly living in the past and either feeling like a victim or longing for the better past times, bemoaning the present as just so flipping awful; OR, we could make use of those times and resolve to survive, move forward, harness the experience and make something positive out of it after licking our wounds.

That's what I want to focus on, the threads and memories that have brought me to where I am now. Every story, memory and event has a purpose. So I hope you don't mind me sharing some of those experiences with you. I promise there IS a point. One part of the very long point being those memories have been the thread in my self-reliance journey but I can't promise it won't be dull. That's entirely up to you.

Right here I'm warning you that I'll be flitting between past and present a bit here and there. I'm confident you'll be able to keep up though.

Going back to the title of the chapter, my own Lightbulb moment came in 2019 as I said. Moments of illumination and realization are a consistent thing for me, moments when you stop because you need to or because circumstances out of your control force you to. Those are precious moments disguised as flipping annoying ones.

I think I cover those moments of reflection a bit more in chapter 3. For now I'll simply say that those moments can change the direction of your whole life…or sometimes just the day.

Either way, things will never be the same again. Life can be such an adventure! Who said adventures are all fun and magical? They are full of dangerous and scary moments that take us out of our comfort zones and ultimately bring us to newness of whatever nature. The outcomes sometimes depend on our attitudes and responses to them. Responses or reactions will result in either a tragedy or an inspirational story. Obviously I hope this is an inspirational one. So let's move on then.

3
REVEALING FOUNDATIONS DOWN MEMORY LANE

I don't like reality TV type programs and game shows normally,except for the ones in our area of interest as long as they aren't like those sensationalised rubbish things for views. I can't stand soap operas either and have never understood why people want to spill all their personal lives and dramas out for the nation or world for entertainment. The reason seems to be an insatiable craving for public attention and celebrity.

That said, I DO enjoy learning about subjects from people who share their experiences to teach or help others. After all it was the 'New Life Abroad' programmes that inspired our own dreams. That's completely different, more on that story in a bit. I love to visit likeminded peoples' YouTube channels sharing their highs and lows in our similar topics. I'll list some of my favourite channels at the end of the book along with other resources I've found valuable.

Even if we on social media and YouTube have very different lives and situations, we have common interests. Learning from them has helped me get along in my own journey much faster and with fewer mistakes than if I didn't have these people for my examples.

As some of you already know and as I have mentioned I do have my own YouTube channel but it's a small one with only a few subscribers to this date. Obviously it's Blue Garden Cottage. I share what we do in our home and garden in relation to suburban homesteading with Permaculture principles and some of our projects.

I would love to do more and join those channels in inspiring others to get closer to nature, be more self-reliant and find joy in what they DO have. So it's inevitable that I need to share a few things with some personal details, but only relative to those subjects.

This is where I get a little less comfortable and a bit more revealing of my thoughts and memories. I'm not comfortable sharing personal info or history but they are after all the foundations of now. So let's go back to the beginning. No, not that far. Just to my childhood somewhere in the mid to late 70's. Ok, maybe that IS way back.

You'll notice how gardens keep coming up (I wish I could use an emoji here too). Just imagine a laughing face. One of the first memories I'm sharing with you is of two little girls making mud pies in the garden and eating them pretending they were tasty desserts.

I remember my friend's name was Seva. They were either Portuguese or Greek but the family name suggests Greek. It was a long time ago! Anyway, I remember by her back door an older lady, possibly her gran, sat plucking feathers from a chicken. I'm surprised now that I didn't think much about it back then. I was only little and loved animals. It was just one of those things. We lived next door to each other.

In our house at that time I remember cold mornings walking to school on frozen dry yellow grass crunching underfoot and seeing two little songbirds frozen solid to the fence... obviously dead. That really upset me. It's so weird how that bothered me and not the dead chicken.

Those were early connections with nature that stuck with me.

In that same house, I remember a flood that came through the house. I don't remember if it was a natural flood event or a manmade consequence but it seemed to be knee high for me. I was practically knee high to a grasshopper! (That was worth at least a smile.)

Anyway, other memories connected with that house were my mum's rockery, cooking and both parents' artistic talents.

My dad painted landscapes with oils and my mum was a sketcher. I loved colouring in. I suppose that's where I got my creativity and love of arts and crafts from.

Fast forward a little and my parents were divorced. So you know,at that time in South Africa, where I was born, It wasn't automatically the mum that got custody. More like who had the secure living accommodation job and finances even if not the best culture or attitude around family.

When visiting my mum, she always had a little something growing wherever she was unle4ss she lived in a flat. One house she lived in had a big old range cooker. I remember her cooking Hubbard squash grown in the back garden with their nobly dark green skins and giant lime shapes. Mum often made pumpkin fritters which we loved sprinkled with cinnamon and sugar. Yum! That gets me drooling. I want to go make some right now!

The next memory is probably not really one for going into too much detail. Imagine an L-shaped annex built on the back of the building connected to the garage. There were two rooms joined by a 'bathroom' block in an L shaped building. The room doors opened up to the outside with no covered path between them. The separate toilet and shower cubicles had corrugated metal doors with gaps underneath. Lovely in the summer, blooming horrible in the winter! That might sound like hell but I was a child at

15

the time and thought it was a real adventure, except in the winter. We lived there when visiting my mum.

Mum has this talent for making a home out of practically nothing. She could make a tent feel like a Tardis or one of those tents in the books about a certain teenage wizard. She made hand sewn curtains, bedding and clothes and even made wire cars for my brothers with long steering poles so they could run around the garden with them.

She could make a delicious meal out of very little too. Mum still amazes me. I think that's where I get my love of homemaking from and my ability to scrimp and scrape and make do and mend.

Every home she made felt like a playhouse to me. I loved being at mum's even in the most humble of settings. I'm sure as an adult, she probably hated it. I could feel the love she poured into everything she did so to me it was all so magical.

My grandparents had a lovely house. In SA most people had bungalows better known as single story or ground level houses. Only wealthy people had double story houses. I tell you what; I would love a bungalow now.

Anyway, the house was in the middle of the plot so the garden wrapped around it. My favourite part of the garden was the back garden. There was an orchard of peaches, plums and I think apples and pomegranate trees. I think quince too.

Along the boundary fence at the end of the garden was a row of prickly pear cacti. I loved prickly pears! There was this huge loquat tree too which we climbed and free ranged under as children.

Along the side of the house there was a wide border with shrubs and flowers connecting the front and back gardens. It ran opposite the kitchen and dining room. We would sit at the kitchen table and watch the birds come to feed on that side of the garden. At the end of that stretch of garden you came to the front garden, bordered up to the front low wall with trees and shrubs.

The big front garden was my granddad's collection of roses. Well it looked like a collection because every rose had its own bed...and there were loads, all in a perfectly manicured lawn. That must be where I got my love of roses from. There was a veranda to the front door too and I remember a creeper, probably Ivy giving it privacy. I loved that garden and I know it had a huge impact on my life.

Their neighbour we called Aunty Betty (of no relation. It was just the way we spoke to the older generation). She was a very British lady. As children we referred to her as 'English'. She had an orchard too with lovely gardens but different. That difference I now know to be a traditional English Country Garden.

The feel of it continued in her house with very different decor from what we were used to. It was simple, clean and homely but delicate and again what I now know to be English/French in style.

There were shelves in the kitchen and I think a pantry filled with bottled fruits in syrup and jams. I'm sure there were other items too but those fruits in syrup, oh my days!

Ah, I'm drooling again. The images of these two gardens, homes and of my mum's homemaking have obviously influenced my own love of those topics and my whole life.

Your patience here is appreciated and I've only two more memories to share in this section that help to set the foundations for the rest of the book and the Lightbulb moment this whole thing hinges on.

Mum's talent for scrimping included her ability to budget with pennies (or more accurately Rands and Cents in SA). I remember sitting next to her as she pencilled onto a piece of paper, all the commitments of debts, rental and bills, then what was left had to fill the kitchen and bathroom cupboards and meet every other need. Of what was left after the 'have to' commitments were met, she would write down all needed and wanted, then scratch out the least important until it all fit into the cash available.

That was my first example of extreme budgeting. Hubby and I are lucky enough not to have to live quite that strictly even with our limited budget. Because of mum's example, I know that if I needed to, we could survive and thrive on less than we have now. What mum did with what was essentially pocket money was amazing trickery to me. And in the 21st century now we have those nefarious organizations hell bent on destroying cash for CBDCs... That's another story and you can tell I'm no supporter.

I even remember her making papier-mâché hand puppets for us. For someone who had a bit of a dysfunctional family upbringing with little example of motherliness or homemaking from my gran, mum was and still is amazing! Love you mum!

I have to add that Gran, we called her Ouma, was lovely in her own way but was a working mum and wasn't very homey. Mum proves you don't have to be defined by your past or stick to what you grew up with...unless you want to, and in my case, I want to. I have one last example of my mum's influence and my interpretation of it, promise.

This time in the mid 80's as a young teen. My brothers and I visited my mum and step dad in the mining town where they lived for a while. I think it was near a town called Knights. I'm not even sure of the spelling. My step dad worked in the mine there and I have no idea what sort of mine it was. I was a teen and that kind of detail just wasn't important. What was important to me was the home.

I remember a terrace of corrugated tin houses. My mum remembers brick walls and definitely corrugated roofing. In my memory the bathroom at least was a metal building, funny how time can warp memories.

The mine houses were terraced single story rows and there was dust everywhere. I don't even remember tar roads being everywhere, except on main routes. My brothers and mum might remember it differently. Mum remembers making the wire cars for my brothers in the garden of that house but I remember them playing with those wire cars in my grandparents' garden.

The interior was obviously insulated. In those temperatures both winter and summer would be really bad without it in tin houses, or even single layered brick walls for that matter. As per usual, mum could make a home anywhere.

I remember playing games from a games compendium with my brothers in the living room. The bedrooms had the same kind of feel as the rooms in the post-war prefab house at St. Fagans Museum of Welsh Living in Cardiff, if you've ever seen it. This memory is the reason that the prefab house in that museum is my favourite there.

I don't remember much about the garden. I'm sure there was a wood or coal store for the range cooker, I vaguely remember. I think there was a pigeon coup as well. That could have been a different house. I don't remember there being anything in that garden growing, just a courtyard.

The kitchen and bathroom were my favourite spaces. In the kitchen, I think there were a range cooker and an electric cooker. My most precious memory of that place is the homely feel between the decor, cooking and baking mum was so good at. She made the most delicious sweet milk rusks and stews in that kitchen!

I mean, you can tell by now, that house had even more of an effect on me than Aunty Betty's house!

The bathroom was an extension from the kitchen and really felt rustic. Mum made shelves out of wooden tomato crates and her hand sewn curtains hung on the window with stretch wire.

I think there was a curtain around the sink and a rug on the floor. There had to be. The bathroom had a solid bare concrete floor. I remember sitting in the bath with the smell of apple scented shampoo and there were candles for light. All this and the warmth of the water made it a magical room to me.

I'm sure that's why I dream of a plot of land with a single story corrugated tin house. It's also why every time I pass a corrugated tin building or old tin church I can't help but remember and dream.

The memories I have of these things may be incomplete and as I said, remembered differently by other family members. That's not important. What is important is the effect my own memories have had on my journey.

These are some of the memories that have touched my soul and influenced what I have grown toward over the years; probably because they are attached to good emotions.

Instead of longing for the past though, I have tried to take the best parts of it onto my present and future. A love of nature, gardening, humble homemaking and creative crafts, all became threads and fibres of my being.

My mum wasn't an outwardly religious person but she had a belief in Christ and in a very basic way taught me to trust and believe, have faith and pray, and follow my conscience in the way I live. It was the beginning of spirituality for me.

Going back to the mining house and my age at the time, there followed the next teenage stage as is normal where those memories were consigned to the mental filing cabinet and I fumbled my way into adulthood.

I had found or rather it feels more like I was led to a man different to all I had ever come across. It was as though our meeting was part of a plan. Even though we were from completely different backgrounds and cultures with different experiences in life, we just connected and within a year and a bit were married. I was 18 at the time.

Considering the different trials and events of our lives, it was amazing that we ever met at all. More than thirty four years down the line and I'm so grateful we did meet.

A year later we were expecting our first child and since hubby's parents had moved back to the UK, we followed and I emigrated and immigrated. He followed almost 3 months later. I felt at home in our new life and country and later discovered that I had Welsh and Scottish ancestry too so maybe that's why.

I didn't settle into married life so easily. Who does? The lessons of my childhood came back without even thinking about it and they helped me fumble my way through marriage, work and family life for both of us. Looking over it all, I don't think we did too badly, all things considered.

In almost every home we lived in, there was a garden. Our children used it generally as children do. I soon discovered Gardeners' World on the telly and got the itch to grow. Our first attempt was just maintaining the already established garden to the front of the house. In the back garden was a strip of soil next to the hardstand we used for a driveway.

We planted potatoes there, just to try it out. OH! I tell you what, that first harvest was soooo magical and we were hooked! Our allotment experiences followed. Mostly negative but I had the bug so what do you do?!?

It wasn't long after that there were programs on the telly. You know the 'New Life in the Sun' ones I mentioned earlier. People packed up and began a new life in Europe, going off-grid and running smallholdings or other businesses.

Our hearts soured and we both yearned for The Good Life. That's a British sit-com that we absolutely loved. If you ever get to watch it, it's a hoot! The couple, Tom and Barbara Good, who lived in the suburb of Surbiton (no idea if that's a real place), decided to turn their home and garden into a suburban 'smallholding' and make it as financially efficient and productive as possible aiming for self-sufficiency. OK, Tom was a rather chauvinistic character and much of the humour was a bit inappropriate but my focus was the ideal of escaping 'the system' and living off the land.

With no experience, and doing things the traditional way through trial and error, it showed the raw and hilarious as well as heartbreaking triumphs and failures of that 'good life'. It didn't put us off and only fuelled our desire for that lifestyle even more.

By now we had a mortgage and hubby was doing two jobs. I quit full time factory shifts and work, for part time work to look after the family and home. We dreamed and plotted how we could have this dream come true. It wasn't to be.

Remember that hydra I mentioned before? It was there, lurking in the shadows around our life and threw us a curveball that smashed the windows of our dreams. An accident at work which led to numerous x-rays and tests, led to the conclusion that hubby would not be able to work again. Not due to the accident alone but historic traumas to the body, never found in the past. There's more about that in later. That didn't sit well with him.

We grew up in a culture and country where if you didn't work, you were out on the street or dependent on family. Work was the ruling principle. There was no social welfare system there and no National Health Service iether. However, in the UK at that time, we had no choice but to fall into 'The System' (Otherwise called the dole). We had to sell the house because the welfare system classed it as assets and would only pay the interest for a year. The 32 year mortgage would still have to be paid at some point. So we sold it. There was no other alternative at that time. There was only a tiny amount of equity in the house but I go more into that later on in the book.

It meant moving into a social housing property which was our first experience of renting a house from a housing association.

We took it as an opportunity to learn and work toward our dream. Books, programmes, and activities such as foraging, gardening and preserving became our pastime. We studied John Seymour's Book of Self-Sufficiency and began turning our garden into our little Eden. Because of physical and financial limitations, frequent hospital appointments, operations and treatments, that took us a whole five years.

In those five years, we became familiar with the nature of the dole and the need to get off it was obvious. By that time we got the garden as we wanted and it produced really lovely veggies, flowers and we even had four chickens for eggs.

We would sit in the summer evenings outside, just listening to nature and watching the bats flutter overhead and across the sky to the nearby trees. We lived in a neighbourhood almost surrounded by countryside. It was the closest we had yet come to the dream. It could have been tempting to just resign to it.

The pull and opportunity to move to Wales from England came along and we decided to grab that chance, with both hands! It was stressful and a huge upheaval but we did it. Within two weeks of arriving here though, I felt completely at home. The rest of the family took a bit longer to settle.

That's a blooming long 'bla, bla, bla', but please hang on a little longer. Those early foundations were still at work at that stage.

We had moved 3 times more before getting to the house we're in now. Still in social housing and we're still very grateful. We DON'T intend moving anywhere else unless the sale of books and other creations earns us our independence again.

Life moves on, children grew and one moved out before we moved to this house. In social housing you are housed according to need so there was no need for a third bedroom and we were moved. Downsizing filled us with dread because we knew losing a bedroom we would also lose a room downstairs. Crazy that. It never made sense but that's just the way it goes.

From the outside, the house we were to move into seemed much smaller. We could see through both living room windows that the back garden was small and had a cypress conifer hedge. Nightmare! But beggars can't be choosers. We accepted and moved.

Things often look worse than they are in the beginning and after a time, it turned out that the house was actually perfect for us. We don't have to go through the living room to get to the kitchen and back garden anymore. It's a separate room instead of a through road. The kitchen was just as small but had more possibilities for creating space. It doesn't have the backdoor straight into the kitchen. There's an extension to it with a walk-in shower and toilet. Brilliant! A second bathroom...luxury!

Both the front and back gardens in fact, turned out to be way bigger than the other house and even though the back garden is a slope, it was a blank slate then with loads of promise and possibilities!

The upstairs has a smaller bathroom but two large bedrooms...no little L-shaped box-room. Oh, and a window on the landing. We soon shrunk into the house and have made the most of it...not done yet. It's that 'glad game' thing finding the silver linings and counting blessings.

Here it was possible to settle. I just HAD to make it home like my mum used to and I got stuck in. The garden took on quite a few changes until 2019 when it was almost exactly where we wanted it with just a few more projects to do. Actually we keep coming up with more projects and in reality, it's an evolution.

There's still a lot to clear out and put in order in the house but I can do that now. It's our home. It only took four and a half years to get to that point in this house! Its funny how finally settling can bring you to a pivotal point.

Until 2019, it felt like we were being driven by something else. There was no more drive to move. Calm before the storm? I wasn't aware of it then and just got into the swing of daily life.

The usual running around after family, going to medical appointments, caring for vulnerable family members, planning our self-reliance and crafting was what we did. Boring I know, but that's when crazy things happen. That's where the Blue Garden Cottage journey actually jump started.

Oh my goodness, you deserve a badge for sticking it out!

That is the turning point. The foundations are set, here comes the Eureka moment. In fact it was the first Eureka moment that has led to many more. It's been a roller coaster ride ever since.

4
A WAKE UP SLAP AND NEW DIRECTION

Remember I mentioned times to stop take stock and reflect? It was exactly one of those times, thinking of memories and dreams that led to one of the biggest Lightbulb moments of my life. That Lightbulb moment that brought a whammy of a turning point. Before I tell you about it, there's just a little more stage setting to put up with, promise.

Our gardening habits have changed and we have learned so very much. It was 15 years by the time we moved to Wales and had 15 years of beginner amateur gardening experience. Both in the garden and the house, we have learned to make do and be creative to reach our goals of a settled life because after all, the 'Good Life' dream abroad wasn't an option anymore, more scarcity mindset talk.

While in our previous address, I became aware of edible landscaping and growing unusual plants for food courses. I jumped at the opportunity. It was like a key turning and opening up the secret garden of my mind. Those courses led me to Permaculture and obviously with no money, I studied all I could on YouTube and from books.

After moving to this house I found Permaculture Association Wales and on their website found a PDC (Permaculture Design Certificate) course. All the other courses were 2 week live-in courses and way too expensive. That didn't fit in with our family needs and wallet. But one course stood out.

It was in Bristol run by Shift Bristol. Once a week on a Thursday evening over 12 weeks with a number of day trips on a few of the weekends sounded perfect. There was a concession and I could pay it off. How could I not jump at it?!? It was meant for me.

The PDC was amazing and I met so many wonderful and different people. I also learned that Permaculture was more than just the way we garden and could be applied to every aspect of our lives.

It opened up new views and options for connecting with nature and people and how we interact with them. It even connected with all my foundations to give us something to build on that would make the dream a reality, just in a different way.

HOWEVER, that hydra, beast of a thing! It was still there and every time we thought we found a way out, it blocked our way...again and again. The hydra's biggest and most annoying head was the system we were trapped in (More on that later). How were we ever to escape and how could we even dream anymore?

Have you ever felt like that? Your dreams forever out of reach, you give up (or so you think) but the yearning is still there. You dare to hope and try again...and give up again. So you keep going and at the same time you keep longing and looking for any possible chance. The rinse repeat cycle starts again but as I already hinted, not forever.

Hubby had taken up making walking staves as a form of pain and mental health management and by the time we moved it had morphed into whittling.

Our house was becoming crammed with wooden craft items over the two years. A friend suggested selling them. We tested the market for a couple of years and only did a few Christmas fairs each year.

It took all year to build up stocks because of the pace at which he had to work and because we had to take money out of the housekeeping to pay for materials needed. Each year, tastes changed and it became difficult to predict what would sell. Along came 'Brexit' and people were not spending in fear of the financial consequences and all uncertainty.

It was clear that the crafts would never be a breadwinner and the orders we got were not really enough to keep him in wood, tools and supplies, let alone make a profit. We would keep crafting anyway at the pace he could manage just for the sake of his health and keeping his mind and hands working as long as they could. Of course also to keep our home from being overcrowded in crafted wooden items. Much as I loved them, there was no space to store them.

I would keep painting and finishing the items just to build up stocks until there was enough or until we ran out of money from the housekeeping to fund it. Here comes the wake up call.

So there I was in the early summer of 2019, sitting in my new 'studio'. A shed really, but set up for a craft painting studio. If you go onto my YouTube channel, I have a video about the setup of that studio and then a video talking about this wake up moment.

Anyway, I was painting the wooden characters he had whittled. It was a lovely day, quiet and peaceful. I could hear the house sparrows chirping and squabbling in the hedge behind the workshop. It was one of those moments when I just had to stop and rest my eyes from the intricate detail of painting.

On my desk was a placemat I had kept from years before. It had an image of a walled country farm courtyard with pretty climbing roses around the back door and a few animals (pigs, ducks, chickens and a collie dog) with an apple tree. It was a romantic representation of the old dream.

I forgot I had even kept it. Holding it in my hands, I wondered what it would have been like to have that dream of land, countryside and 'the good life'. Oh well, maybe it was just as well, I thought, staring out the window.

I don't know what happened in my mind at that very moment but I must have been taking stock of what we didn't and did have. Depending on your situation, idle pondering can be dangerous to your mental health or life changing for a better thing.

Staring at the placemat image, we certainly didn't have livestock. We have a dog and wild garden birds. We didn't have land acreage...hang on a bit.

There in front of my eyes as I looked up out of the studio window, was the circle of apple trees I had planted to grow a kind of domed folly. In some way, we did have an orchard. There were fruit bushes everywhere around the garden in pots. I had roses dotted around the place too. Still do. And there at the end of the garden attached to the house is our veranda. The outside room we wanted, to be able to sit outside in all weathers and enjoy nature.

I'm sure that when I say I looked at that scene and then at the farm image again and out into the garden again, you can imagine that I was still trying to process it.

Looking over the other side of the garden, there was his workshop, a cherry tree and a kind of fruit cage of sorts. Three mounded no-dig veg beds (now raised beds) and food growing in them. Then there is the 'potting shed' of sorts again.

My mind travelled in through the back door into the entrance. Above the door and all around the hallway were shelves of food storage. In my tiny kitchen was the dehydrator and other bits showing preserving, fermenting, and yet more shelves above doors with food storage.

Storage is a problem in tiny spaces, obviously. In the front garden, the fledgling cottage garden and herb garden full of promise are already producing crops.

In the living room with its make-do, up-cycled and charity shop finds along with items gifted by friends and family, was the evidence of those childhood foundations.

With my mind returning to the present in my studio, looking at that place mat yet again, and then the garden again (I really was going back and forth), a light flicked on in my mind, "How the heck and when did that happen?!?" My heart was pounding and my mind was reeling.

I mean again, talk about being slow to connect the dots!!!

All those years of dreaming, longing and planning

And those foundational memories, courses and experiences and here we are. Euphoria filled my being and painting crafts completely took a back seat. I just sat there amazed. The biggest smile on my face ever! We blooming well have the 'Good Life' as in a darned good version of the old dream.

So what now? I mean the realization came like a slap in the face. It was like the 90's Tango soft drink TV advert I mentioned earlier in the book, where people taking a sip of the fizzy drink were randomly and magically met with a bright orange tubby guy who gave them a slap in the face and instantly disappeared with the slogan…'You've been Tangoed'. That's exactly how I felt!

Even now, just writing about it, that memory gets my heart beating. Lightbulb moment? More like a glaring headlight moment!

And that was it. "You Numpty!" I thought to myself. All this time we were already living the dream in portions. We hadn't just been gaining knowledge and experience that would help us manage when we finally got the dream. We were subconsciously making it happen all along the way.

Isn't that the way it goes really? If you want something bad enough you will make it happen no matter what.

You might say compromise. I say it's a matter of perspective.

So what now? What do you do once you finally click that the dream is now a reality, even if not quite the way you dreamed it? For one, we certainly don't have the lovely Mediterranean climate! We do however have the gorgeous green of Wales. As I'm sitting here typing away, I'm listening to the Shire soundtrack from The Hobbit, thinking of the Welsh countryside and hills. It makes the heart sing. Well I can tell you the rest of that day I couldn't do much at all. That was a high point with spectacular views and I didn't want to come down.

What I DID do the next day was read and write in my 'business plan' journal from years before and began to figure it out.

Because the longed for dream wasn't lurking in the back of my mind anymore, I could focus on a new direction. It was time for a new adventure.

I wasn't aware of that hydra still there in the background. It would take a new plan and determination not to merely navigate those obstacles but climb, hop or jump over them, whatever it takes. So, what DO we do NOW, was the question.

Health issues were worsening and that hydra was still at our heels, throwing constant obstacles and walls in our way.

I suppose the subconscious beginning of the change of perspective actually began at the beginning of 2019. When I found that quote from Don Campbell; 'If you want to make minor changes, change the way you do things. If you want to make major changes, change the way you see things'.

The quote struck a chord and helped to change how I think about what the dream actually is and how I can make it a possibility and a reality even in our situation.

The change and challenge was actually fitting the dream in with what we have instead of getting what would be needed to make the old dream a reality. Let's face it, neither of us is physically fit enough to handle the physicality of a smallholding or farm right now. I plan on changing that by the way. After accepting that I needed to change the way I see things, I got on with exactly that...changing how I looked at the situation. That's an abundance mindset thought.

Look, accepting your situation and changing the way you see it is NOT a cop-out. It's NOT giving up or settling for less. It's about making the most of what you have and making your dreams come true, even if there's no money or opportunity to make the original dream come true. I feel deeply that we can sometimes dream big and that's good, but now can be even better than the dream. Especially when you have been single minded in your goals and the present passed by without you even noticing.

You can go a whole lifetime chasing a dream and completely miss noticing what you already DO have the dream. That would be so tragic. I have a lovely ornament hanging on my wall with the thought; 'Some people look for a beautiful place. Others make a place beautiful.' Now that I have what I wanted in a way, I want to make the most of it. I want to do what my mum did in home making.

Honestly, even now, more than four years since that moment, just thinking about it still fills and lifts my soul. It was the moment that cemented my BIG WHY. The motivating and life changing core of what I do and want.

Such a big event can sometimes have a downer of an anti-climax. It can be unsettling. Not for me. It was the opportunity I had wanted alongside and part of the dream to be financially self-reliant again. I wasn't going to let being stuck in 'the system' get in the way of me figuring it out. That's another journey I'm about to share with you. How DO you get unstuck from socialwelfare?

5
FIGURING IT OUT

For the rest of 2019 until November, I poured over my old journal entries, not quite a proper business plan but more like an idea put into order. The business of plotting what I needed to do to make it work began. The 'business plan' I put together 2 years earlier and my 'annual review' of goals for the year held more possibility of becoming a reality. New Year's Resolutions are NOT a thing for me. It was time to turn this realized dream into a workable part of our self-reliance journey.

I started by figuring out our What, Why and How. Well, I already figured out our WHY. Actually, the why is evolving and changes with each progression but the main core and thread remains the same. Look out for more on that later in the book. What we are and what we do, and how it would move us forward in our financial self-reliance goals was the new adventure.

Of course the most important questions then were what and how? There was no point going anywhere with it until I figured that out. There are so many things we do and all are part of the one. What's the one?

We are crafters and already know that the crafts on their own wouldn't buy our financial freedom. It would never be more than a hobby that would pay for a few projects.

Are we gardeners, allotmenteers or farmers? Not farmers and definitely more than allotmenteers and gardeners.

I am an author, homemaker, appropriate prepper (another book to come in the near future on that topic). I would love to be an instructor of sorts on all of that.How do I put all of the above into one category? How do I connect them all? Maybe I need to figure out the purpose or more accurately, a new WHY? Like I said, keep reading.

By August I started to check out the differences between smallholdings, homesteads, cottages and cottage gardens. The original dream was a smallholding or farm with a cottage garden look and feel. It has evolved into something more. What is the 'more'?

After a lot of 'surfing', I printed off all the info I could find on all three (smallholdings, homesteads and cottages with cottage gardens). With neon highlighters I set about highlighting every word or phrase in each that applied to us specifically. I have a video on that too. THAT was an eye opener!

Firstly, it turns out the technicality of a smallholding is a land based business focusing on animals or crops, or both. It can be a market garden, or a CSA (Community Supported Agricultural scheme). It is smaller than a farm and can have anything under 50 acres of land. WHAT?! I've always thought a farm is anything over 10 acres. You learn something new every day. I think some Americans call it a hobby farm. Totally different to what WE do and we definitely don't have acreage or livestock. So scratch that one.

Moving on, Homestead was next. It's more of an American term and dates back to the 1862 Homesteading Act in America. The details of that can easily be found on the internet so I'm not going to bore you with that. Instead, I'm interested in how that term evolved to be what it is today. Originally it was about settling and subsistence living for a period of time and cost consistently as stipulated by the act and then the 'steader' would own the land.

Of course over the generations the term homesteading came to mean not just subsistence living off the land to own it, but also to include what was done IN the home connected to the land, using the traditional hand-to-mouth and survival skills.

It evolved further to include crafts, homemaking, preserving produce from the garden plants or animals and even a small business.

That evolved further and later to include suburban settings too. Well now THAT sounds just right for us!

Gardening to grow our own food, crafts, homemaking and writing/working from home...and anything else we can do too. So homesteading sounds just right...but that's not all.

Going onto the Cottage and cottage garden bit, because I always wanted a cottage and changing the way I see things, I wanted to make my home a cottage. Of course! Why not?!?

Just like Homesteading, Cottage has evolved from the stereotypical idea of a countryside dwelling with thatched roof and surrounded by countryside. It became more of a romantic idea to include the cottage garden and the lifestyle of those living in the house.

Further down the line into the present, on a technicality a cottage is generally a small dwelling of 4 rooms. Remember the term '2 up-2 down' to describe a house with two bedrooms upstairs and two rooms downstairs (kitchen and living room), on either 1 or 2 levels. It could be extended for more space, detached, semi-detached or terraced, and not necessarily have a thatched roof nor does it have to be in the countryside or even have a garden.

'Cottage' has evolved into more of a romantic idea of the lifestyle of those who live in the house and the style and feel of the home. A lifestyle now referred to as 'Cottage core'.

Well now THAT sounds just perfect to me too. We have a semi with 2 up and 2 down. The feel in the home is going toward the feel of cottage homeliness already.

As to the cottage garden, well summarising all the highlighted bits were; informal in style, mixture of edible, useful and ornamental plants, with a mixture of traditional and modern plants. It generally has roses for a staple. The cottage garden has natural materials like wood and stone including arches and is enclosed. Now let's just compare for a minute…

We have all the above descriptions of plants including roses (and I have 10 so far. More to come), there are edible, useful and ornamental plants, and wood for the fence and pergolas, and stone dotted around and arches. Both front and back gardens are essentially enclosed and informal. It's cozy with a 'secret garden' feel. Still lots to do but the bones are there.

Brilliant!! It's what I've always wanted! There we go again. So on a technicality and idealistically, we can legitimately call our home a homesteading cottage and garden.

Oh, and we also use Permaculture principles in both. So a Permaculture homesteading cottage and garden is exactly what we have. Oh wow, what a revelation! I need a moment before I carry on…

So, where does the 'Blue' bit come in then? Well, for years now a pattern has emerged in our home and lives. I started to see blue items and themes everywhere I looked and nothing was planned or designed. Nothing was deliberate. Looking back 32 years there was even blue in our wedding clothes and decor.

I even took photos of all the blue bits gathered together oh, and was that freaky?! I decided that if it was a natural theme in our lives, why not make it deliberate and begin to include it into the style and design of both the home and the garden. Create a brand if you like.

Now that we know what we do and are as far as property goes, time to figure out a label, niche and 'brand'.

I already have a YouTube channel but was so unhappy with the name for almost a year. I mean, 'The Permaculture Shoestring Home and Garden' was such a mouthful that people referred to the channel as PSHG...It definitely had to go! That was the first thing that had to change. There's more on the planning and plotting a little later.

I checked out a few names on the internet like Suburban Homestead...gone. It didn't say anything about 'cottage' or 'Blue' anyway. The next one not available was Blue Cottage....REALLY!?!? Suburban Cottage was also gone. Because of the title of my first book, My Shoestring House, I thought maybe The Shoestring Cottage...Nope, gone!

My life-saver friend who always comes to the rescue when I strike a blank suggested Blue Garden Cottage. At first I couldn't see it...probably because my head felt like there were nursery school children banging on all sorts of items for 'musical' instruments in my head with so much going on in it. Again it took stopping, breathing and visualising... Of course she was right. It was perfect!

It was also available on domain names. I bought three variations. That's all I couldn't afford. No really, I paid money I couldn't afford.

Love it! Stop, take stock, visualize and with help from my bestie, ping! That's another Lightbulb moment, happy days. Time to bring out the eco-friendly party poppers and streamers! I know. It's sad but I finally got it!!! Like I said, I can be a bit slow on the uptake.

Everything was unfolding perfectly. So now that I know WHAT Blue Garden Cottage is, it's time to figure out the biggie; the new WHY? I think I've hinted at that regularly through the first part of the book already but there is a more practical reason.

6
WHY THE WHY?

Without a WHY the next chapters would be useless. Let's take a look at the importance of the WHY.

'Why?', can be either a word or a whole question, depending on the context of its use.

Can you remember ever hearing a child ask a 'why' question and they question every answer with another 'why'? They repeat the question to every answer until you get stumped for an answer and just say, "Because I said so!"

That can be frustrating because you realise you don't have all the answers and you're the grown up. I suggest a better answer might be to admit you don't know the answer to that one but can check it out, even better, investigate it together. I can offer the suggestion now only because it's what I wish I had done. My grandchildren have benefited from that lesson as far as their questions to me go.

That's not the type of 'WHY' I'm talking about. I'm talking about the kind that motivates or prompts your decisions. OK, let me give you an example.

"Why bother with breakfast today?"

Scenario 1; "because I've been up since 3am. It's now 8am and I'm starving. Cuppa and a cookie will do for now".

Scenario 2; "I have an important task to complete today and I really need some energy to do it so I'll have a good breakfast".

In the first scenario, the why was because (I've) been up for ages and am hungry. It's a quick fix to an immediate want and leads to poor choice of breakfast and hunger again within half an hour.

The second scenario was an example of a more compelling why. There is something important depending on me for completion and therefore my choice of breakfast needs to be one that would help me to physically and mentally do that properly.

The 'WHY?' is our motivation and reason for the goal or task. If it's not based on something really important to us, it won't be enough to help us progress toward the goal. The bigger our goal, the more compelling the reason needs to be and in reverse too, your biggest reason will influence your goal, ambition or task.

I've had a number of big 'WHYs' in my life but I never actually thought of them specifically nor have I been aware of them in that context. Maybe it's because I only ever considered the difference between the want and need, then put the need ahead of the want. I think I was still finding my perspective spectacles then.

There have also been a fair few wake up calls that have scared me enough into some big why ponderings. I have already shared all the foundations with you and they have been threads in my desires, goals and personality but they aren't compelling reasons. If they were, I'd have had the land and lifestyle by now.

I think I have also already mentioned our motivations for wanting to get off social welfare and work on our self-reliance and self-sufficiency. That was a big reason and my foundations steered the direction we went. But the biggest

REASON and MOTIVATION for wanting change was fear. Really it should have been something far more positive.Fear is a scarcity mindset motive which just invites more scarcity. I wish I knew that back then.

Yes, we got part time jobs in between the times on benefits that were supposed to be doable but no, the wages were pitiful and we still had to have top up benefits to manage. So no improvement financially and worsening health. If I haven't already mentioned that, it's in a future chapter. I think this stage is what changed our wants and desires into needs compelling enough to become not just ambitions but goals.

I ask you, what would trigger you into major change? Let me share one of my major pivot moments.

In 2010 I was working for a well known home and garden hardware come department store in the UK. I was a supervisor on the twilight shift. I would get up by 5am, see to the house, family, dog, work on the allotment, served in church callings, help my very young teen son with his paper round my daughter settle into her own home.

Life revolved around all the usual day to day activities of family life that normally would leave no room for a job as well. Then by the time supper was prepared, I would go to work. Work was 17:30pm to 23:00pm. By the time I signed staff out and locked up to go home it was 11:30. I'd get home just before midnight.

After almost a year of this type of routine, I noticed on my way home at almost midnight that I was nodding off into micro-sleeps for just a second but it was enough to suddenly feel the car veer slightly and jump back into awareness. My heart would race and I really struggled to get home.

THAT was a huge wake up call. It really made me afraid of dying and leaving my family on their own let alone traumatising them for a job that didn't even pay the bills. I think you'd agree that's a compelling reason for major change.

Something HAD to give and the job was it. I think I talk a bit more about this in another chapter but it's relevant to my exploration of these compelling reasons for massive change.

After the AWAKENING in 2019, It was important to decide where to from there. I've already covered that so will spare you. It's enough to say that since my not wanting to die driving home at nearly midnight episode, my big reasons have evolved.

The biggest reason for any and all of what we do used to be our longing for freedom and security.Freedom not to have to report to or be accountable to anyone and have our every moment analysed and dictated. We have had enough of having to account for every little difference in routine in our bank account.

Ok so that'll come to everyone in the event certain world dominating agendas actually succeed, but for now I'm referring to our need for finding ways to provide for our needs and wants, our financial freedom and future without being told, how many hours we can work or how much we can earn or save. We would love to be totally independent and that's what we are aiming for.

We want to live, save and dream on our own terms and without any restrictions except those we put on ourselves and minding our example to our family.

The way things are looking nationally and globally for the future of our children and grandchildren are motivators strong enough to evolve those goals to also finding ways to make a good living and show our children and grandchildren how to become resilient and adaptable not just for their survival, but for them to thrive. I don't want to survive. I want to thrive and be abundant. If we are abundant in both life and finances, we could help others too.

For now, I'll focus my big why of building financial, mental and spiritual resilience and freedom.

I hope so far that you've begun your own awakening of what you have and want in life. What's YOUR WHY, your main reason for change? Write it down in bold lettering andhang it where you will see it every day.Make a point of reading and repeating it out loud every day like a mantra.

I'm going to take you back to that time of self-assessment after the awakening and all the plotting and planning to make it happen. I had to figure out WHAT work I could and would do to make that a reality.

With clarity, energy and a new direction, it was time to put pen to paper, get planning for the next stage and move on with a new beginning…

7
THE MAGIC OF PEN TO PAPER

I don't know about you but I just have to get my plans and goals down on paper and then just like a puzzle, put them all in order so that doing the first automatically leads to the next and so on. It makes for a much smoother task, takes less energy and helps to get more done quicker. Then I can actually feel a sense of achievement and completion.

There've been so many unfinished 'jobs' around this house and garden for so long that now we have the opportunity and having moved them from the to-do list onto the doing list, things are being completed. The chorus line from Flash Dance, the movie pops into mind... 'What a Feeling!!' Hang on. I need another moment to compose myself.

My oldest grandson thinks it's hilarious that every time we use a phrase that was used in a movie or song, I sing the phrase or line in the tune. We have a lot of giggles. He calls them cringe moments.

I wouldn't say I'm obsessive because nobody could ever accuse me of being a clean freak. Don't get me wrong. I would love a tidy house but not a sterile or minimalist one. Even so I like to tackle the housework, gardening, crafting and writing with a plan. Just because there is so much to do that I normally tackle them all and never complete any.

I discovered Kan-Ban boards. The best one I have seen is from Heart Breathings, Sarah Cannon on YouTube. She's an author too but in a different genre and very successful. I was inspired by her board to help me make actual progress. I took her idea and adapted it to our needs.

Of course in true shoestring style I used what I had around the house, a cork board, blue fence paint and loads of ribbonny bits, glue gun and string.

Excited and chuffed with the outcome, I then discovered that post-it notes won't stick to fence paint. Typical! I settled for drawing pins (thumb tacks) and post-it notes. In the end, it's the principle that matters most, more on that in the Plotting Tools chapter.

Online kanban board equivalents for those who like things techie are available but I'm a hands-on crafts person. That and I don't have time to keep checking my phone or other tech.

It's sad I know and it gets worse. Since completing the edible landscaping and PDC courses I just can't pass a garden without designing it in my head. It's ridiculous! Of course you can't go design a garden without observing over a period of time and considering the needs of the household it belongs to but as I see it at that instant in passing, I'm mentally visualising it.

I do the same with the rooms in my house and in the garden but then I DO have the opportunity to observe and properly list resources, obstacles, needs and the usual SWATS.

'Experts' say that readers, followers, viewers and so on, are NOT interested in YOU, the writer, vlogger or whatever. They want to know what you can DO FOR THEM or what problem you can solve for them.

They also say that you need to position yourself as the expert and you do that by story. People generally use well known stories or parables but honestly, what story holds more power? One you re-tell about someone else or one you are personally connected with?

Seriously, the most powerful stories I have ever heard have been peoples' own stories told with all the emotion of the events. Those stories stick with you. So how can I NOT tell you my story if I want to get a point across or relate how we overcame obstacles to make our dreams a reality and share it in the hope it would help or inspire someone, somewhere? That's why I get a bit frustrated by what some of those 'experts' are saying. It seems contradictory.

One of the experts I came across who didn't confuse me at all was Andy Herrington. I've never met him and have never been to any of his seminars but I did buy his book, Passion to Profit. I found it very helpful and inspiring. Still working through it and by the time this is written and published, I probably still won't have finished it.

I've gone off on a tangent again but it's relevant. I watched loads of videos on the topics I needed to learn, to make things happen. For more than 7 years YouTubers living Permaculture, homesteading, prepping and homemaking are what filled my 'spare time'. Yep! Sometimes I have to check my diary to remind myself what those words mean.

Alongside vlogging, IT, marketing, online course creation and writing for online publication, I also watched loads on how to create videos... I still haven't got most of it to make sense in my head and think I will struggle with it for ages because I just didn't have the IT skills and equipment for it or the time to watch ever more. My viewers and readers are very patient.

Since writing this first time round, I've bought more tech and learned more. I have actually started podcasting and have my first one up on a number of platforms. Hopefully by the time you get this book, I'll have loads more.

Going back to my mum's example of budgeting, I think that had a big influence on my need to plan and put things in order to be able to make them work.

I don't know what I would do without pen, pencil and paper.

It isn't very eco-friendly but there is just something so, how can I put it? To me, there's something spiritual and magical about putting a pen or pencil to paper and letting my thoughts trickle out of the end of the pen to become something physical, not just an idea, plan or design in my head. It wasn't always like that.

Memory alert!! Back in primary school my handwriting was so bad that one of my teachers assigned another girl in my class to show me how to write neatly. Her name's Anne. I first watched her. Wow! She had a hand so skilled it was like seeing printed calligraphy. I was spellbound!

She showed me how she used different pressures on the up and down strokes and an imaginary line in the middle of the row for the lowercase letters. I really wanted to write like her and practiced with every chance. It quickly connected with my creative roots and the ink flowed as I learned to write in cursive. It must be where my love of actual writing comes from. Sometimes it just takes a different learning or teaching method to connect with something you already know and I think I have always been a spiritual person. If it connects with my soul, I will grasp it.

Writing was like conducting music and still is. I feel being creative is a spiritual activity. Creativity (especially in nature) connects our spirits to this incredible and awesome mortal world and beyond. You know, I would even go so far as to say that writing could be a form of meditation.

The pen becomes some conduit between my mind and the paper. In this particular case, the keyboard has become my pen. I can pour a little of my heart into writing, infusing the words with the emotions and thoughts in which I recall what I'm writing.

Sarah Cannon chose the name for her brand, Heart Breathings because of a quote from William Wordsworth. "Fill your paper with the breathings of your heart". That's exactly how I feel about writing. It's the breathings of my heart. Well, any form of putting pen to paper. Writing, drawing, painting, colouring, sketching, and even budgeting and planning, it's all the same to me.

As time passed from my childhood, writing became a necessity rather than a pleasure because of time restraints. That's why it's now such a treat to me. I mentioned that I have a journal, well I actually have 2 and a number of diaries and calendars for each 'thing' I do.

My personal journal in which I write every few months or if there is something really important to record. The others are for the record of Blue Garden Cottage; for the crafts, writing, creating digital products as well as the social media channels and pages,a kind of business diary/journal. The writing's going to need a separate diary of its own. I also have a garden diary.

Connected with that weirdness is my love of stationary. Seriously again, I've got pens, pencils and all sorts in boxes as well as the school exercise books my children never filled completely in school. The used sheets were torn out and the empty books kept. They've come in handy so often, I can't count. Paper is precious! ...and I hate waste.

And books! I have a small library in my house, about 4 tall bookcases full of reference books, course books, all things homesteading, preserving, DIY, crafts, religious and all sorts. You won't find any novels except for a few family story books, scripture and manuals. Oh, and the Permaculture or smallholding magazines given to me by my friend, which have specific articles relative to us (and my favourite home magazines kept for years as I only buy about 2 a year max).

Writing everything down and putting things in order, has helped Blue Garden Cottage homestead in becoming what it is now. It's still a work in progress but at least a reality.

We actually have the dream and we are living it while it's evolving. I can't stress enough how just saying that makes me feel.

That's in part, the power of pen to paper. I don't want to bore you any more as far as my love of writing goes. You get it, I'm sure. The whole purpose of jotting things down in this journey and then sharing it with you is that I hope it will have some value for you.

Going back to the obstacles and opposition in realizing dreams, even with all the planning and preparation, the hydra still keeps making its presence known. My weapon is 'the plan' and cunningly side-stepping the beast where I can legitimately and legally, to build reserves slowly so that when the time comes we won't be starving ourselves to make it work. There's more on that too later in the book.

There IS an escape plan, and I want to share it with you but first I want you to know a bit more about that hydra...Well, our hydra anyway. They're all so individual. Of all the heads of opposition it has, the biggest one is 'the system'. Not quite the capitalist, consumerist system. That's one of the other heads. I'm talking about the one I mentioned in the foundations section,yep, the dole or social welfare system.

I'm sure everyone who has ever needed it has had different experiences of it and the system itself is continually changing. That's one of its horrible and equally, potentially good sides.

Another disclaimer here... What I share with you about the UK social welfare system is based on our own experiences over the past 20 years and because it's constantly changing, will probably be different by the time this book gets to you. Everyone's experiences may be different.

8

THE HYDRA'S MEANEST BITE

Warning! This is a long chapter. Brace yourself.

When I say I'm going to share our experiences over the last 20yrs, I don't mean 20yrs continuous dependence on the system and I'm not going to give you 20yrs of history either, I promise. That would be torture even for me! By now if you are still reading this, torture may be exactly what you've got... and you paid for it! Seriously, I'm impressed you're still reading. I really appreciate it.

Growing up in the 70's and 80's, people of my generation were force-fed the traditions and social hang-ups of the previous generations that personal finances are private and you don't talk money with anyone else, especially children. I recently found a meme that read, 'Tradition is peer pressure from dead people'.

Generally, men wouldn't even discuss it with their wives. Others left it all to their wives to deal with and didn't want to know anything about it and heaven forbid money matters should ever be discussed with their children! That's disturbing. Oh hang on, that still happens today. Children don't get the benefit of advice on how to manage budgets or money as they grow, let alone what being an independent adult means with paying bills and taxes and then looking after themselves and family, if they have one.

No, I don't mean giving children scary tales of what it means to be an adult. I don't mean the 'money doesn't grow on trees' spiel either. Don't even mention all the other negative narratives about how hard it is to be an adult and how hard you have to work to make a pittance or that money doesn't even pay the bills. Been there and done that. It's never good. No wonder our children wouldn't want to grow up! That negative mindset stuff is lethal to young minds and their futures.

Instead, I'm talking about sharing with them the tools and techniques of successfully living independently, meeting responsibilities and still being happy and having fun, because once we have done the 'need to dos', the 'want to dos' are so much more fun.

Let me just add in here that I'm not saying that we can't have fun until all the HAVE TO DO's are complete. I'm simply saying that is a point of prioritising immediate needs. It IS important to find some fun, entertainment or pleasure in between all the immediate needs or we will have that negative and scarcity mindset about those important things. Sometimes, the fun things helps to keep you focused on those important things. It's the oil in the lamp thing.

Getting back to the money matters in relationships, I have seen couples where a spouse who handled all the red tape has died and left the remaining spouse to try to figure it all out by themselves only to end up in a financial mess because their finances weren't a joint concern while the other was still alive. How cruel is that?!?

In the high school I went to, Youth Preparedness (YP) classes were compulsory. In them we learned about personal finances, personal and home care, car care, and even choosing careers and universities or college. Not a clue if it's part of the curriculum now. It should be.

Thankfully my mum took every opportunity to teach me, especially by example how to budget and look after myself by her example. I'm ashamed to say that I haven't always followed her example and have paid the price for it. At least I have her example to fall back on. She also taught me that every job was of worth; even the most menial jobs and we always pay our responsibilities or bills first and then use what's left and don't go over. I've already covered that in the foundations section so won't bore you with yet more. On some level, that in itself is a step toward the scarcity mindset but it's a valuable tool when it comes to managing your finances.

For my purpose here, it's enough to say that I was taught the value of money in different ways since childhood and I am glad I chose to follow examples of frugality, resourcefulness and creativity, especially now.

Sharing personal finances with and teaching my children was difficult, not because I didn't want to but because our children were of the 90's. It was boring to them. Society in general in the West, had this idea of preserving their childhood and not burdening them with that kind of stress. I didn't agree and felt that it didn't have to be stress nor boring. They took the narrative of negativity because managing and exercising self-management were dirty words.

Of course by the time they're teens you don't stand a chance. That chance has gone and generally speaking, we can see the consequences today because charities dealing with debt and financial crises are stretched. Not just from people dealing with current economic impacts but like I said, because lots of people just haven't been taught in their childhood homes and it's not generally part of school curriculum.

I don't think even my own family will be immune to what's been forecast for at least the coming years as far as global economies go which we have no control over. That includes the effects of wars and threats of war in other parts of the world because of our global interconnection. I think or rather hope I have built enough of a foundation for my own children to help them figure it out and more than survive. Time will tell.

The social welfare system here was stretched and tested to breaking point when as of December 2020; there were 370,000 people officially unemployed due to Covid alone. And that's not counting the Elderly, disabled and those on very low incomes who need top up benefits.

A system under that much pressure can't last, can it? That's something hubby and I thought when we first came to the UK in 1990 long before Covid was even thought of. How could such a system survive?

We were so fortunate for him to get a job within days of arriving here. It's what we did. No job was beneath us. When we saw the stereotyping of people on the dole back then, we knew we never wanted to need it.

We had good foundations of work ethics and money management but most people aren't exempt from unexpected crises that force you into situations where you HAVE to accept defeat and then be very grateful that we DO actually have that kind of system.

The money system, generally in the 'West' basically works like this; you leave school, college or uni and get a job. It's the way our capitalist society works. You get a job, pay your taxes and National Insurance which the government uses to manage the country's finances and 'look after' its citizens (and line their pockets). Well that's what I understand simply so far. You are a part of 'feeding the machine'.

Of course the governments of countries also take out loans from the World Bank and others like the EU organisation when we were still part of it, basically an EU Dole system getting the nation dependent on it.

You, the citizen, spend your money with utility companies and other businesses as a consumer, which also in turn feeds the economic system. As does all the money we 'earn' and spend.

The problem is that the economic system depends hugely on getting people into debt...well, not specifically. It's about making money on interest and speculation of investments which is gambling with someone else's money...ours.

The money we pay in taxes (income, duties, VAT, property, inheritance and more) doesn't add up to the money the government pays out in so-called expenses.

National Insurance is supposed to be a kind of savings for our pension years and to cover our medical costs to the NHS and then also for the social welfare people may need in times of crisis between jobs...not even thinking about the disabled or elderly who's pensions are totally not fit for future costs of living.

That tiny percentage of money we pay into the NI (National Insurance) scheme, will never cover the amount of money we take from it in our entire lifetime because life is NOT that predictable and you can't just go from one job to another in days anymore...unless you're very lucky (or you have a very abundant mindset and you are totally in tune with the law of attraction. Life changes the things you are able to do over time and the cost of pensions, care, social welfare, doctors and hospitals all cost a fortune! Our local council tax is supposed to cover education, emergency services, waste management and parks and leisure.

The nature of economies and what makes them spin changes too, so factory jobs are replaced with IT jobs, call centres and retail. Retraining is expensive and only covered by social welfare in certain circumstances. The funding you get for retraining is classed as income and therefore deducted from your total benefits.

I just don't get that, seriously. It's more of a deterrent to retrain because of course a person's going to give up paying bills for months to get training for another job that's probably not going to improve their wages and they are then in debt anyway. I think not.

Now remember that we are talking about UK social benefits here and according to my family's personal experiences.

Because we have an NHS (National Health Service) treating us 'for free' at the point of service, most of the nation don't have a clue how much their visits to the doctors, dentists and opticians, or their treatments actually cost.

We take our pets to the vet and 'flip our lids' about the costs. How on earth is that tiny proportion of our NI contributions going to cover OUR needs? It just doesn't.

That's some of the many reasons why governments borrow money from international banks and put their countries into debt...I have 2 words for debt... financial slavery.

We get into a spiral of increasing interest and taxes to cover the debts and costs. There is a way to reduce costs but it's not popular. Don't even get me onto the outrageous salary system for not just politicians (higher ranking of course), and managers in business...let alone investors. It infuriates me that politicians are quick to get rid of the NHS but not curb their fringe benefits and wage rises that have nothing at all to do with inflation!

For one, top politicians and local governments do NOT need almost £100K and more a year to 'survive' and then on top of that, get a 'hardship fund' AND their 'expenses' paid...Seriously!?!? I mean ok. Let's not go there. There's a risk of a rant here. I can feel my blood pressure rising. OOPS, too late. Take a deep breath... exhale, moving on.

That whole system was bound to reach a point where it just can't go on. I think we're at that point right now. That's why my husband and self could see all those years ago that it surely couldn't last.

We have our politicians coming up with ideas to 'improve' the health service which is code for what has been planned for years...getting rid of our NHS in favour of private healthcare which in the UK would be a disaster.

You would go to the grave with hundreds of thousands of pounds of debt if you are fortunate to live to old age. People are already beyond stretched with finances let alone being able to contribute to private medical aid schemes for every member of the family.

I love the principle of our welfare system and our NHS. They are the life-saver of so many, including our own family. It is something we have to protect but we have to make sure it is fair, dignified, compassionate and practical, and well funded without plunging the country into more debt or selling the health service off to foreign contractors as many departments already are, we just don't know about it.

It's definitely not the NHS I have a problem with. Nor do I have a problem with the social welfare system. They both are vital. What I do have a problem with is the politicians and their puppeteers who use it in such an unethical way. The system traps people and has total control over them. It is a gateway for 'them' to get you trapped into the agenda of 'own nothing and be happy' and the universal wages even if you are in work. It's the sinister side of it that worries me. The original principle of the system itself is a wonderful one that looks after us in times of our most vulnerable stages.

The way the system is implemented and distributed is imperfect. Ok, so it's impossible to have a perfect system when it's programmed and run by imperfect humans and is open to imperfect interpretation as well as being changed at the whims of political leadership and maybe a little corruption too. I lose count of the changes brought in over the decades by politicians to 'make it fairer' and prevent or catch those taking advantage of it who shouldn't.

Every year qualifying criteria and rules change and DWP (Department for Work and Pensions) staff can hardly keep up with it. DWP is the title of our social welfare system. In reality, the restrictions and policies they wrap the system up in make it incredibly difficult to get off once you are there. At times it is a contradiction in that some who really need it just can't get it.

Then there are the social stereotypical attitudes toward people who depend on it. It's generally presumed that people on the dole are there because they want to be, are lazy or have no education, ambition or morals.

I suppose TV programs like the sitcom Bread from the 80's just fuelled that kind of attitude. Reality shows fuel the attitude too and yes, there are some families who have for a few generations been dependent on the dole, who are trapped there not just because of the habit, but because so much has changed in education, costs of retraining, and the fact that despite government spin to 'make work pay', work doesn't cover the cost of living, let alone pay the debts society demands to fit in with the Western lifestyle. And I'm talking about the 'need' to upgrade constantly even when you can't put food on the table.

Personally, I don't care about trends. I don't go for upgrades of anything unless the tech I do have (phone and laptop and podcast equipment. That's it), become obsolete and can't be updated or have broken. And that's rare.

Rant Warning.

I do not understand why people who are struggling financially think it's ok to still go on holiday, feed habits like drinking and smoking (not to mention others), get new phones or gaming equipment and software, branded clothes or anything branded for that matter, when they say they can't afford to put food on the table or the things needed for their children for school.

I'm not saying everyone does that but I can understand the bias and stereotype we are all labelled with when people see that. That's what makes me fume. Media of all types including social media like to portray all 'Doleys' as freeloaders, scroungers and liars.

Just to clarify, I'm not interested in keeping up with trends. Like I said, I value my freedom. So much of our freedom is already stolen by politicians and dependence on financial help that we lose something of ourselves. We lose our dignity, ability to manage finances and daily life and even relationships. What I mean really is that to be in need from the system, you have to give up your freedom and dignity because they examine every aspect of your finances, personal information, your family situation, the lot. We lose our self-reliance. By that I mean our ability to provide for ourselves and families the necessities of life and security.

It's the nature of the money system. For those lucky enough not to need it or those who do but can't qualify because of crazy requirements, wages stay the same or go down while costs increase. There are some practical solutions we can all use to even out the difference and I talk more about later on in another chapter.

With everything changed to online applications, reporting, and communication, if you are broke and don't even have a phone, let alone a pc, laptop or tablet, how do you apply for benefits and jobs? 'Go to the library' they say. Sure, there are computers you can use for free in our local council run libraries but you have a limited amount of time you can use it for and forms, online or on paper, take hours to fill in. Library opening hours are also limited. Even looking for a job, all things are done online now. Gone are the days where you could hit the pavements and hand a CV to prospective employers. Everything is now online.

You rarely get face to face appointments unless it's to report on progress in job finding and the way you are held over a barrel, so to speak. In fact, since first beginning to write this, the system has changed to even more online accountability. It has become a sterile one size fits all system without the human ability to reason individual situations.

What about the elderly or disabledand those who don't have any tech skills? Librarians don't have the time to sit with people teaching them how to use these tools. It may be the 21st century but financial means and skills decide who can move with it. As I said before, people all have different experiences and some may even have good experiences. Our own are mixed.

Going back to our experiences, I mentioned before that my husband was fortunate to get a job within days of arriving in the UK. It was factory work and he really didn't mind. We love work. It was and is still part of us. I couldn't work for at least 12 months due to immigration requirements and I was expecting our first child anyway.

By the time our daughter was 3 months old, I had been granted permanent residence with permission to work. Back then, my husband had to prove he could support us without help for 12 months even though he was and is a British citizen before I would be granted permanent leave to remain in the UK. That's perfectly reasonable and right. We didn't want to claim benefits anyway and were happy to carry on as we were raised, by making do.

Once I had permission to work I took part time work in a retail shop working on the tills. There was a lot to get used to in a new country and culture but work helped.

My mum-in-law (a Brit living in the UK and whom we lived with at the time) looked after our daughter while we were at work. It didn't help that I went back to work when she was so little. If I knew then what I know now, I would have stayed home until she had gone to high school.

By the time our son was born I had opted out of work to look after our family better and hubby took extra work wherever he could. He was eventually doing 3 jobs and it took its toll on his health. I mentioned a work accident that set the ball rolling with his health investigations.

By the time our second child came along, we had a mortgage. It's what you do after all in any capitalist Western society. You get a job, get into debt and are owned by the money system, working to feed it. If it's not one 'system' it's another!

I'm sure you've had enough of a travelogue of our experiences up to now but this experience serves to back up the WHY for wanting to be self-reliant.

It's enough to say that life changing events forced us to rely a few times on the benefits system. It was a curveball which circumstance had thrown at us. This curveball was not so much a slap in the face of independence but rather a punch in the gut. It was even more of a cultural shock than immigration! What on earth were we going to do? He was told to quit work if he wanted to keep going (looking back it begs belief). He was told that mostly because he was wired for mechanical and hands on work and was really good at it. There was no internet available to Jo-public unless you were stinking rich and had a spare room for the size of equipment needed back then, let alone the skills to use them.

I didn't have any qualifications that would pay the mortgage, all the bills and feed the family. There was no option but to sign on. I can't begin to explain how humbling it was.

We ended up having to sell our home. The house sold and there was a tiny £3,000 equity which fell below the threshold of what we were allowed for savings on the dole.

Tell you what though; we still had to produce receipts for every penny spent of that £3k to prove we didn't have savings. It wasn't hard as we had just moved into a house that needed carpets and decorating and paid off a tiny debt.

That was our first realization of what was to come in loss of freedom, financial self-reliance and dignity. It was already a double edged sword. On one hand we were so grateful to have a roof over our heads, food in our bellies, clothes and no debt. On the other hand, we could see us having to pay a really heavy price for the privilege. Obviously that's as it should be.

There was this split personality to the system. It took regular visits to the housing trust, jobcentre and medical consultations to regularly report on conditions and progress to see if we still qualified.

Of course, that's how it should be but it was the attitudes of some who worked in the system that made it a negative experience. I mentioned this before. You were made to feel like a scrounger, and a cheat, met with presumptions of laziness and wilful avoidance of work. It was obvious that we had to get out, but how?

We moved from England to Wales and we got everything transferred over. The problem was we had to rent privately because moving to Wales was classed as 'choosing to make ourselves homeless' and didn't qualify us for housing immediately but we could be placed on a waiting list. Fair enough. There was a points system for housing based on need and the same still applies now.

The need arose as the accommodation became much more difficult to manage with physical limitations and the children were getting too old to share a room. The continuous cycle of proof, changing qualifying criteria, changing needs, house moves, Re-assessment every 3 to 5 years and even finding work in between which was supposed to be doable for the condition (but wasn't), meant life was one big roller-coaster ride.

I really don't see how some people can refer to living on the Dole as having an easy life. It isn't. Yes you are given money and can barely live on it but there's a heavy price and nobody really would actually choose to live off it permanently if they have other choices, or rather, if they were aware of them.

It's that lather, rinse, repeat cycle of life that was sucking any possibility of freedom, self-reliance and dreams out of us. Please understand, I'm not complaining. It could sound like a complaint from the outside listening in unless you have been through it.

As I said, I've always been grateful for the privilege of having a home and needs met by a very generous system but it's not meant to be there for you forever unless you are elderly or disabled with no possibility of ever being able to change it. It's ridiculous that even the profoundly disabled have to prove they still need it and it's glaringly obvious they do!

I know that we were in a situation of need, not out of choice but due to disability. It would be understandable and acceptable to most people for us to accept the situation and make the most of it. But we had dreams and if something could be done to change the situation; we felt a responsibility and drive to do it. If there is a way to become independent again, it's our responsibility or rather privilege to find and use it.

The problem and another side of the hydra's head is that to get off the dole, you need to have a way of making enough money to survive without it or you would still be tied to it for top-up benefits...and the continuous cycle of proof and accountability. Again and understandably, that's as it should be.

It's meant to be uncomfortable so we don't get too comfortable and stay on it. However, if you really are NOT able to work, there should be more compassion and dignity, more recognition and absence of labels.

If you have a change of circumstance and as it stands now, you apply to go onto the Universal Credit (UC) which is only a few years old and understandably meant to take away a lot of the confusion and chaos of having so many different benefits paid at different times. That sounds great.

The UC amalgamates all your benefits into one payment (except those that are exempt, like some disability benefits). This was also to help people on the dole get used to getting a salary and managing finance outside of the dole. The reality is that even off the dole, most people wouldn't be in the kind of jobs that pay monthly. They would be on minimum wage and part time contracts that pay weekly or fortnightly. Few jobs available to the poorer or less skilled folk actually pay monthly.

The principle or intention of UC was good. The implementation was horrendous!!! It has apparently now changed so you can choose to get money fortnightly.

It also allows for limited employment and income without it affecting benefits but if you go over the threshold, benefits are adjusted until you are earning what you would have on benefits matches and is scaled until you are not getting any but you stay on the system so that if you get less than the benefit amount you would get, your wages are topped up to the limit the government says you need to live on which is way below what people actually need.

You will never see any politician living off that sort of money. So if wages are below the limit, then you understand why people say even with national minimum wage, work truly doesn't pay. Looking back, it's still better now than when first introduced.

When first introduced, UC had serious consequences for people when going onto it and if you didn't have a reserve of cash (extremely unlikely on benefits) you would immediately be put into debt to survive.

If you own your own home and need to rely on social benefits, as with us you would be expected to sell it and live off the equity and you won't qualify. That's perfectly understandable and right. No argument from me there.

That's why it's best to have a reserve to live off and insurance in case you lose your job or the like and avoid the Dole all together. If unavoidable, make sure you have a reserve of up to two months' food and cash set aside for just in case while you wait for things to be sorted, more on that later. That kind of reserve can help anyway in avoiding the need for the dole but only if a new income/job is coming before it runs out.

Housing and council tax benefits are normally paid straight to your landlord, which is fine if you are in social housing but if in private rental, it gets tricky.

Private Landlords generally want their money at the beginning of the month whereas Housing benefits are normally paid at the end of the month.

So if you rent your property privately you could lose your rented home too because most landlords aren't that understanding and generally, private landlords won't have tenants on benefit, full stop. So to avoid this you should also aim to have at least two months' rent saved up to cover it as insurance. There are however new laws in the UK protecting tenants from being evicted immediately.

When first introduced, UC applicationstook around 8 weeks to process and it was not an automatic change over. Your benefits were cancelled and you had to apply for it. Some applicants didn't know their benefits were going to be stopped until they got into trouble with direct debit payments not going through to pay bills and not having money in the bank for food.

That was the first they knew about their benefits not going into the bank. Scary if you don't check your bank regularly to see that your money has gone in but if you aren't told, if benefits are stopped and it takes up to 8 weeks to process before you even get a decision…you really do need that reserve and backup.

I sincerely hope it has improved by now. If you haven't already had experience of the system, you should still be able to see how difficult it was and can still be, and maybe understand how some 'complaints' could be justified. I'm not complaining though.

I recently found that there have indeed been more changes still. It looks like there is hope. I'll go into that a little further on. All I can say is that the benefits system is an ever changing and evolving system. Who knows? It may finally someday be something we can once again be proud of.

Until then, I will settle for being grateful that our household at least has been supported by that system. The system is not funded by National Insurance contributions alone. It's at risk, not least from certain political parties and IS an expense that doesn't generate income for the country so is one of those expenses that regularly get 'thinned out' to cut costs. Of course that makes good business sense but the system isn't supporting businesses. It's supposed to support real people on their knees.

I think I have covered enough ground now to give you an idea of just some of the many aspects of the social welfare system and again I stress that I am not complaining and it is an ever changing system so that by the time you get this, it will have changed again. This explains why I view that particular head of the hydra as a real beast.

So what can be done? We can't change the system ourselves and can't always change everything about the circumstances we are in. We could get stuck there. But there are things we CAN do to help our situation and changes we can implement to make it less of a struggle. Going onto the Dole is something that should be a last resort, not a first port of call unless every other option fails. Seriously, It ISN'T a picnic.

There are ways we CAN manage and even thrive. It starts with self-discipline, preparedness and having a really strong reason as mentioned in the WHY chapter.

I'm not giving you a bullet point 'how to' here, just a few ideas that have helped hubby and myself to get to where we are today and some of the things we wish we knew and used before. What works for us may not work for you. Your own circumstances may be completely different to ours.

Whatever changes you have on the Dole are classed as change of circumstances and you will then be put on UC.

I'll repeat for clarification purposes. Once the transition is made and you get settled, even if you get a job or become self-employed, your info stays on the system so that if you don't make enough money or lose your job again, it's just a case of informing the jobcentre online to either top-up wages or reinstate benefits until you get another job (though again, that takes weeks to calculate but not as long as if you are starting out from scratch).

Not so bad IF you can make provision for the initial upheaval by saving up resources while they are available. I go into these more in section 9.

If you have a reserve to last 2 months, you will sail through it. There's just one thing about reserves. If you have any, it should be in the form of food and other storage, no debt and cash reserves because you are expected to live off what's in the bank until you get a new job or run out and THEN apply for help. Your bank balance should be used to pay your bills to avoid getting into debt. At this stage you already have more stress than you would want and having a reserve can minimize the stress of it.

That's fine if there are loads of jobs available but the days of walking out of one job and into another in days or even a few weeks are gone. Unless you have some sought after skills and experience, then you might not be reading this now anyway.

If you CAN live off your reserves AND get a new job in that 2 month period, brilliant! You don't need the dole then and have preserved your freedom and independence. Most people aren't that lucky.

Oh, the UC comes with the provision of a 'crisis' loan you will pay back as soon as your claim has been processed. They take it off your total before it goes into your bank account so you don't have to physically pay it back yourself. It is after all a loan which is a debt. You know by now how I feel about debt.

That means what money you are awarded will be even less than you need to survive anyway. It'll all go back to normal once the loan is paid but while it's paid back, you really do struggle.

The system needs to change and it has in small ways. A few years down the road since UC was introduced and there are still problems but it has potential. It seems the prospect of escape isn't as scary now as it was before but you still need to be able to buffer yourself for the change.

I suppose that even though what I'm saying might help to keep you from ever needing to sign on, it's also meant to help those IN the system and wanting to get out but not knowing how.

For many folks though, it's a bit more complicated than that. Hubby and I tried a number of times to find work that we were told would be appropriate for the condition, a claim made by people with no medical qualifications or acquaintance with the job roles they were presenting.

As a result, the condition worsened further and we were back to square 1. So if you have disabilities, you can't get a job you're able to do, aren't able to retrain and the condition is degenerative, what do you do?

Well the partners of those on disability benefits are sent for work focused interviews to prove why they can't work. I'd think that's obvious...you are the carer for the disabled person. Really?!? That raises the question then, what CAN we do? You know the saying. Where there's a will, there's a way.

With all the changes going on in both the benefits system and in our own lives, there's one thing we CAN be sure of, change. In fact, new info indicates that ALL benefits will soon be included in the UC system. So in the meantime, we have to put our home and finances in order (thankfully we have no debt except for the overdraft) and we'll have to use all the tools I talk about in chapter9.

As I mentioned before, my husband was doing crafts for pain management and we tested the idea of craft fairs but it was obvious it wouldn't pay the bills at all. It was mainly to keep him busy while I found something I COULD do. It would stay a pain management thing for him and we would save what he makes for the odd fair every couple of years just to replace wood and tools. We only ever did 3 years anyway which only qualified as testing the waters.

There was too much variation and uncertainty so crafts are a luxury. Luxuries are the first thing to be excluded from peoples' budgets when hard times hit. Since then with all the changes nationally and globally from 2019, we no longer do fairs. It was back to planning then.

I called JobCentre+ at the beginning of 2021 and explained my plan to be an author and that because of the way Amazon's KDP works I wouldn't get paid until 3 months after the first and every sale, and even then, it depends on what quality I produce and how I promote my books.

They said that I need to inform them as soon as I receive payments over a certain amount and that we would lose the money hubby gets for my support but not his as his is tied to his circumstances.

I can work 20 hours per week and earn no more than the amount stated (that might change over time) then any more than that, they will start to reduce that portion of money according to earnings. That sounds perfectly fair and better than it has been in the past. I'm repeating myself again here.

So because things keep changing, if you are on benefits and would like to make changes, call them first and talk to someone about your situation and what effect changes will have for you but check with them first. You may be pleasantly surprised. I say call but to be honest, You could be in a call queue for up to an hour and still not get through.

We know it IS possible now to get out of 'the system' and just need to figure out how we will make a living. I've given enough of an intro to our own hydra for you to know the beast that kept getting in the way of actually implementing our plans and that's where we go from here.

9
THE ESCAPE PLAN

Over the last 7 years in this house, we have already been on a journey toward self-reliance in a number of ways. Mentally we continue to fight against the urge just to give up and instead motivate ourselves daily to keep going. Having ambitions, goals or plans are a vital part of doing that.

Having goals, ambitions and plans however are not enough. They aren't any good unless you have the intention and drive to implement them. If you don't intend to put them into action, they're nothing but ideas. It's the strong WHY that gets you going.

Back in 2014/15, I came across two magazines. Well they are more than magazines. They were special editions specifically aimed at turning your hobbies into businesses; The Big Book of Crafting (By Period Living magazine) and Turn Your Hobby into a Business (by Country Living magazine).

It's where I got some of the inspiration for how to get hubby's crafts to fairs and out in public. But they're also what inspired me in the garden direction.

Not only were there crafts in the collection but things like niche plant nurseries and garden centres, turningedible flowers into sweets, making fruit vinegars and preserves. It gave me ideas of maybe propagating and selling the unusual edible and useful plants that I grow and use.

Light bulbs went on in my head and my heart soared but for now it was impossible because of the amount of money and space needed to start that up. However, it was the beginning of ideas and planning.

I took the Business Start-up course offered free from Business Wales which was great for the technical and legal information provided but the really it was not much more than a very long webinar to lure you into taking a business loan with them. A course I found even more helpful was the one offered by the church I'm a member of as part of their aim to help people be more financially independent. This course I found far more helpful.

Since then, I've formed new patterns of problem solving to adapt and change the goal as needed to keep it viable in the face of so much change. I wish I was just as flexible physically as I've become mentally.

Not long after the courses, I found an article in the Permaculture Magazine by Arania; Designing Your Permaculture Livelihood (Issue 89 Autumn 2016). I won't go into detail here. I'm saving that for the 'Plotting Tools' chapter 10.

Arania gives ideas on things to consider when assessing what your situation is, what your needs are, how you can reduce the amount of money you need to live off and figuring out how you can create your Permaculture livelihood that would allow you to make the money you need and still have a life.

You know how much I love writing and planning! I enjoyed the process and realized that it was not so much one of those Lightbulb moments but more like a dimmer switch being turned up over about 2/3yrs.

All the different business ideas that came to mind were blocked by that hydra, as I said, because of the lack of money and land, as well as the implications at that time of declaring yourself self-employed and the immediate effect on benefits. For most ventures you really do need capital and you are unlikely to have any unless you are willing to get into debt.

But nobody is going to invest in something with no guarantees of ever getting their money back. And if you don't have a regular income, you can't get a loan anyway unless you are willing to get into stupid debt with loan sharks...which all loan providers are in my books.

Just think about it. Loan providers pitch their motives as helping you when you need it but they do NOT want to help you. They make their money FROM YOU out of the interest they charge for the privilege of enslaving you to them. Great isn't it. You pay them to enslave you. It doesn't make any sense to me why anyone would WANT to do that for anything other than a mortgage, essential education for employment and only if necessary, a means to get to work.

In those two craft to business mags, almost all the crafters had capital and or land to start with. They were employed and did the crafting in their spare time until it grew so much that it took over from their paid employment and they went full time into their own businesses.

No such option for those on the dole or with no spare cash and considering that on benefits you were only allowed £3k in savings before they stopped your benefits. Saving a years' worth of salary wasn't possible anyway. And a year's worth of salary is exactly what you would need to keep you going until you start to make anything near what you need to live off, if your business and management actually grow the business. Then it's no longer a hobby and could drop you in exactly the situation you were in if beforehand you were working up to 60 hours a week.

Arania's planning idea was what kept me planning and adapting, considering what I could do. Along with the

YouTube channels I was following, Arania's ideas helped draw us nearer on the road to homesteading generally. It was a different idea though to the one I had initially and totally different to hubby's dream.

It was during this three year period that I also found the Bealtaine Cottage channel, Rain Country, What Vivi Did Next and Fairyland Cottage, all toward the natural Permaculture and homesteading life.

Collette from Bealtaine also introduced me to the idea of writing about our journey as part of an income stream. I had already published a book (My Shoestring House) as I mentioned back in 2011 but because I didn't have the means to promote and order the book to sell, I put it in the experience file and forgot about it. I was determined never to use that kind of self-publishing again.

The craziness of life continued and we got on with the crafting for pain relief while dealing with family crises. In that chaotic time we completed projects to get the home and garden fully set up and into a settled system because we needed to stop and chill, being worn out with the stress and chaos of years of trying. It was time to stop for a bit.

So by the time the 2019 Lightbulb, slap in the face moment arrived, I had already formed the habit of planning and researching.

I can't remember if I already mentioned Gillian Perkins and other YouTube influencers I found and learned about videography and self-publishing books. All the previous discoveries and learning (and new changes to the benefits system) now made the next stage of the Escape Plan possible.

In this stage of the Escape Plan, the things I did were;

Continue with the two books, Passion to Profit and Ultimate Course Formula.

Plan to create courses. (I will work out a plan for local £5 workshops and free ones as an outlet for selling books and homestead crafts once off benefits).

Plan many more books. (I have another 7 book ideas and the list grows)

Keep streamlining my social media platforms and website.

Complete the website (not really a necessity so that one can wait a couple of years)

Get a printer/publisher engaged while getting the book online first to make enough money to get physical copies to sell (this has changed now. I'll spill the beans later).

Continue to make videos but make them more 'viewable', creating an introduction to the channel and being stricter with regular uploads.

Get better tech to make, edit and upload videos. (Already done)

Start podcasting…which has taken over from blogging. (I have now started as I mentioned before)

I have already created an Etsy shop and have PayPal set up. I just need to make sure the online shop is streamlined with the social media creating the 'brand'.

Sort a logo.

Plan merchandising (I have a few ideas here too).

Oh, and get creating digital online products to sell.

Flippin' heck! That's a list and a half!

The books and courses will focus on different aspects of homesteading in the suburbs and self-reliance. Since first coming up with this plan, I have discovered KDP (Kindle Direct Publishing and other self-publishing companies that DON'T ask for money up front).

This is what I said earlier I would spill the beans on. At this point in writing I already have 7 low and medium content books published, meaning blank journals and diaries etc.

No guarantees of sales but I have been careful to follow advice about sub-niches and keywords, quality over quantity and the Permaculture principle of variety and diversity for resilience. It could take up to a year before I actually make any money. Hopefully sooner if I follow the guidance from those who know and actually make money doing that.

At the moment, I'm working on establishing my publishing business. More on that a bit later so keep reading.

The list above is a long and intensive list of to-do's, let alone alongside the day to day running of the homestead and caring for family, and it will take some time but we have already started implementing them.

Like I said before, I like to plan jobs so that one would automatically lead to another. Now I have a kan-ban board too, it makes things much easier and more achievable.

I have set aside 3 days a week for 'work' and have informed my family of those days so they don't make plans for my time (they really are struggling to grasp that rule). All other days are shared between homesteading, family appointments and grandchildren. Sunday is supposed to be my day off! Not anymore and happily so as there are now three days per week on which we have grandchildren visiting overnight. I have to have at least one day to rest from a full time week. It's my day to heal, rest, and repair and to look after myself so that I can re-energize and prepare for the week ahead. So for now, we have opted for one weekend a month to ourselves for healing and refreshing. That will change as the children get older but for now it will do.

The point is, you have to get into MANAGING your life, your home and family as if you already are a business person even if your self-reliance journey takes you to an online job instead of a business. Whatever you find appropriate for your own escape plan and situation, you have to be self-disciplined and self-motivated. You have to be strong and strict on dividing your work and home hours. There are 'abundance mindset' tactics that will help us all but I think I'll add a chapter on that specifically.

Every trial and obstacle over the years has given us strength, experience, skills, flexibility and resilience. Each one has helped us to prepare for the next level, like those of a game where you win pieces of armour to prepare you for the final level and battle.

So when I said that we have direction, hope and purpose now, this is what I mean byThe Escape Plan.

10
PLOTTING TOOLS

From assessment to budgeting, goal setting and Kan-Ban implementation, this section is where I spill the beans on our roadmap to freedom.

Soooo many times, I tried to draw up the 'maps' I used, to show and give you an idea of what I'm on about. It didn't go so well. I tried to jot the sections down without revealing too much of my personal finances. That was really hard to do because budgeting and planning my way is just what I do and don't normally have to explain it.

Budgeting is the easiest part to start with. As an overview, it's basic and you could adapt it to your own needs. Every home and budget is as individual as the people who live in it.

There are so many different types of budgets that it can be confusing but it's generally looking at a few and deciding which elements of them fit in with your needs and situation or coming up with your own.

For example, we don't have debts (except for an overdraft) or a mortgage and we don't have store cards but we do have loads of 'unexpected' or random expenses. So for us it's important to keep as much money as we can in the bank for those. I'm not going to be a miser or skinflintthough. Hoarding is a scarcity mindset and scarcity invites more scarcity.

Generally, people with IT skills just use a spreadsheet. As for me, you know how I love pen and paper. So it's that, plus a calculator, calendar and multi-coloured pens for me.My love of stationary and lack of skill with spreadsheets for annual planning draws me to an old fashioned method..

For weekly budgets, it's just pen and paper, and my latest bank statement or online banking with my small diary and a calendar.

It's just basic bookkeeping, money in and money out. But none of that can be calculated unless you figure out your annual income first to discover your monthly income, especially if your income is from more than 1 source or comes in weekly, fortnightly or four weekly payments, or all of the above. Calendar monthly payments are so much easier but not the norm for most people in the UK. So this is how I do it;

Weekly payments x 52 weeks = annual income and divide that by 12 = monthly income.

Fortnightly x 26 = annual and again divide by 12 =monthly.

Four weekly x 13 (there are 13 four weekly payments per year) divided by 12 = monthly.

That should help you figure out what your monthly income is.

Now I calculate total fixed expenses; Bank account fee, savings (for opticians, dentists, things that aren't covered by your benefits), Direct Debits and Standing Orders, debts, rent, taxes and insurances). Then changeable current expenses (everything else from groceries, to fuel, outings, celebrations, pet care and gardening or whatever). These suggestions are general. If you are on benefits you may not need to plot rent and council tax if they are paid directly and you may not need to pay for dental or opticians.

I prefer to pay our utility and other bills differently and monthly via DD (Direct Debit). If you don't have direct debits on a monthly basis but pay annually in one big bill, you could make it easier on yourself to divide the annual payment by 12 and set up a Standing Order (SO) to another bank account just for your bills so that you are saving up beforehand and when the bill is due, have the cash in the bank to pay it without going overdrawn or into debt. I believe this is the cheapest way as you avoid standing service charges. Then again, being on benefits, you have to declare every account and are limited to how much you are allowed to save. In that case, you are better off with DD (direct debit).

Personally, I just find it easier to pay by DD even though it includes the service charges. Others still use prepayment meters. This is the most expensive payment method and also includes service charges but at least you know exactly what you are using and won't get any bills. Pick your battle.

Knowing my total monthly income and expenses, I can see if I am living within our means.

If I take away my total expenses from my total income and there is a negative balance, I am living beyond my means and have to make changes.

Once I have my monthly budget calculated, I go to the actual and date specific calendar. Literally I have a calendar organiser.

I plot the dates the money comes in and goes out, celebration dates, outing dates, appointments and projects or whatever. I try to make sure that if there are DD or other regular payments going out before the money comes in, I budget the payments in before that date to leave enough money in the bank to cover it and calculate the dates of the flexible expenses out of what is left and when. That way, I avoid using my overdraft and technically getting into debt, because an overdraft IS debt. I speak from experience that it is so easy to use that overdraft and for some folk it would be better NOT to have one. But if your money comes in irregular payments, it's a safety net against charges if DDs or Standing Orders go out before money comes in.

I do what my mum taught when it comes to the flexible expenses...I fit it into whatever is left after the bill payments. If we keep doing this for at least six months, we should be able to build up a credit balance but as is more common in life, and as parents, little unexpected emergencies pop up.

I try to set aside money for the extras like compost for the garden but with those little emergencies I usually have to reduce the food budget to cover the cost if I really have to. Because I only need compost generally in the spring or autumn, it's not too often.

Just a side note here...my own understanding is that our most important needs include a roof and security over our heads, wholesome food in our bellies, seasonally appropriate clothes on our backs, social connections, nature and a means to provide and protect these things.

As to the 'Self-Assessment' bit, it's basically checking to see if you can change suppliers for cheaper but still great deals to reduce bills, get rid of unnecessary payments or find a provider that will amalgamate a number of services and therefore fewer bills. However, sometimes there are so few differences between suppliers it's hardly worth the effort.

I found one that gave me a deal on combining gas, electric, broadband and mobile phone contracts in one and I saved £70 a month. That is, until the energy crisis happened. Still not recovered from that and we are with the cheapest provider in our area.

Ok, so the mobile phone contract is not that great with limited minutes, texts and data, and the broadband is only the second fastest deal but the point of the change was to reduce outgoings and get out of overdraft. It worked.

Then we got back in again. It's like a blinking revolving door!

I also made changes to the timing of Direct Debits. The amount spent on groceries is usually the only and most flexible money and this expense is altered and stretched according to need, just like mum demonstrated.

When it comes to grocery shopping, I always go through the cupboards, freezer and fridge making a list of things that need replacing instead of buying randomly, forgetting some things and buying too much of what we already have.

It helps to have a store cupboard of staples I can buy in bulk like legumes and whole grains, soy milk, flour, sugar and so on. The basics also include herbs and spices and other condiments that can turn those boring ingredients into tasty meals. You choose what is best for you but the most basic of needs and for survival are generally;

Grains (rice, oats, pseudo grains like quinoa, millet, amaranth and so on)

Pulse (lentils, beans and peas as well as all kinds of seeds)

Seasonings, store cupboard staples like stock cubes and spices, oils, sugars, etc)

Essential toiletries and cleaning products and first aid supplies)

Don't forget pet food and so on.

Add whatever else you think you just can't survive without...like chocolate! That's because even though food storage is normally for emergencies, I like to build food storage so that I can spend less time shopping, less energy stressing if things don't work out, have more resources to share with family if needed, save money to spend on something I really want... The list goes on but in an abundant mindset instead of a scarcity mindset. No doom and gloom SHTF prepping here. Only appropriate prepping.

I'll go more into this in another chapter.

Living out of our food and emergency storage works. As I mentioned earlier in the book, we grow as much food as possible in our garden and hope to learn how to grow all year round according to the seasons as well as introducing more perennial vegetables and growing our own seed not just to stretch our money but also because we want to be closer to nature, to a connection with our food, connection with the seasons, the health benefits of growing your own (mental and physical), and just because I love gardening!.

Our daughter has a couple of streaming subscriptions which she shares with us. Many providers are clamping down on sharing as it's doing them out of business. I know a lot of people say to get rid of streaming subscriptions but if it's cheaper for you to do that than to go out and you don't go over your budget? That leaves funds for the occasional proper outing which makes the outing all the more special. We don't watch that much anyway because the homestead, work and other projects take up so much time. That's another thing...work.

Being busy stopsyou going out for anything otherthan deliberately planned things. Again, that means that saving from not going out will give you an opportunity to go shopping for something you love without the stress of feeling guilty. It also keeps you too busy to stop for lunch then there are only 2 meals a day. There's a cuppa with fruit for snacks if we get peckish. So we tend to eat early and no later than 6pm. It helps to keep your food in a 10 to 12 hour window of any 24 hour period. That's been proven to be very beneficial to health. Whole foods fill up more so forget the low carb fads. Seriously! Eat loads of veggies. Both are generally the cheaper of the food groups and if eaten as whole foods and cooked without all the additives and oils, they are NOT bad and will fill for longer. Obviously change according to your own needs baring allergies in mind.

We also happily accept second hand clothes from friends and family or go trawling the charity shops but only when absolutely necessary, only because time spent shopping is less time enjoying my home, garden and family, and writing.

When it comes to gifts and celebrations, We DO make an event of them but Make do and craft are the general rule. To make a meal of it, so to speak, cook a favourite meal and decorate the table and put on some music, dress up and hey, presto! You have a dinner date or an afternoon tea with home bakes and snacks served on a table setting with room decor is always special.

I think we've forgotten how to make do in general because of the fast pace of life and work and convenience has been great but it doesn't help when cash is strapped.

Christmas deserves a chapter on its own. I love homemade decor, gifts and traditions that really make the season bright and merry. It takes months of planning and preparations so it can be affordable and done before the season starts. You want to enjoy it after all and not slave the month away! Maybe I will just write another book specifically for Christmas on a Budget.

These are just some examples of what WE use and they are individual to our home. There are loads more and maybe another book on make do will be a good thing too. I can go deeper into the details then.

I'm sure you could probably find loads of other ways to make savings in your own budgets. Some things might feel too restrictive but keep the end goal in mind and sight. Keep your WHY visible.

There's nothing like taking control of your finances and resources to help you feel a sense of peace and reassurance. Taking control will help you concentrate on other aspects of coping with extremes. That's one less thing, right?

It's essential right now with a global recession threatening (already here and there always is in my opinion). It's been threatening for years on and off.

Debt always makes it harder to endure but getting into a habit of frugal living will make it easier to cope IF ANYTHING financially challenging ever happens. And that's the point exactly. Live NOW in a way that will buy you security later. On its own, 'prepping' for the worst is a scarcity mindset thing. It actually creates more scarcity. Adapting your WHY to positive outcomes with gratitude can turn that 'prepping' into an abundance mindset shift and actually create abundance.

Another important part of the analysis (self-assessment) is the taking stock I mentioned earlier.

This is where I use the tips given by Arania, mentioned before. His article was generally about self-assessment to discover how you could reduce your need for money so you can take a job that may pay less but give you more hours to actually live. He covers creating resilience by finding multiple and seasonal streams of income to keep some security if one or two streams dry up or slow down for any reason.

He gives examples and a list of things to consider in your analysing. I took those lists and graphs and adapted them to our own circumstances. I hope that's what you'll take from this chapter and other parts of the book. Make what you will of it for your benefit.

It starts with my journal and plans, hopes and goals I work constantly on new ones as needs change. This happens once at the end of the year and I revise again at least in the middle of the next year. I've mentioned Kanban boards before and I use the same categories on my board as in my 'plan'.

Basically, you make vertical columns for your category headings like house, garden, family finance and work. Yours will probably look different according to your needs and situation. Divide the board into three horizontal rows.

The top row is called the To-Do block, next down is 'Doing' and the bottom row, 'Done'.

The top biggest row I divide into 4 week rows because I have so much to do that it would need a whole wall if I tried to plan more than that! You take your tasks that need doing and depending on when you want to achieve them, place them in the week you need to do them. From each column for the day or week, pick 3 and move them to doing.

That's where you concentrate on what's most important, one at a time.

As they are done, move them to the 'Done' row. I promise it's much simpler than I make it sound. It sounds a lot, and it is, but that's what I do to be able to manage them all.This tool helps us to get things done. I have a video about my Kan-ban board on my YouTube channel called 'I'm The Boss of Me'. I am hoping that in the future I will be able to minimize a lot of the things we do. I guess that depends on how far we get with the financial self-reliance goals.

I keep in mind the Permaculture principle that the problem IS usually the solution. It's that whole changing the way you see things that makes the difference and ideas come flowing in.

I made spider graphs and tables to see what worked best for me...In the end it was a combination of all the ideas and examples from all the different people in my life and on the internet. These are foundations that have helped me to get to a stage where I can move forward.

My every day is also plotted generally. It only takes a moment. I can now see what needs to be done every day and adjust where needed so that the most important things come first and I keep flexibility. It's so easy to micro-manage every aspect of life to such a rigid degree that you could snap if overwhelmed by things that creep up and you can't fit it in. You also risk forgetting what IS most important.

I do give myself a whole week in December for yearlong planning and then a day each month to sort the most current stuff and then a few minutes in the morning. The daily list I write, read and commit to memory but go with the flow of the day too. I only think about it again the next morning. Whatever I missed the previous day goes onto the next day's list in the right box of importance if it's still important. It's a lather, rinse and repeat cycle of a better kind.

Did I mention where I got that idea from? A friend shared a tactic of hers for sorting what is most important? Divide a piece of paper into 4 blocks. In each block I write; Important and urgent (1st), Important but not urgent (3rd), Not important but urgent (2nd) and Not important or urgent (4th). Well that's how I remember it.

I'm not going to give you all the boring details but think about it, I get up any time between 3am and 5am. So I start by studying, meditation, and doing quiet jobs. Writing is one of them. All day is busy and by the time I drop into bed, it's anytime between 10 and 11:30pm. On a normal day, it's 5am till 10:30pm. That's a lot of time but not much when you have 4 to 5 areas to your life and all are important.

That said, I intend to simplify my life completely and reduce those areas to their most basic and important elements.

Like I said, now that I have a system sorted and it's working for now, we may be able to drop off or change some of them in the future.

You could spend a lifetime on the internet searching and finding so many different ways of budgeting, planning and organising. The danger is that time will slip through your fingers. I'm not going to make suggestions because to repeat myself, your situation, finances and abilities are unique to you.

You probably already know of many more effective ways than mine. For now this works for us. I hope you find what works for you. "Each to their own", as they say.

It's been many years in dreaming, learning, finding planning systems and budgets to get this far. It has taken changing the way we both SEE and DO things to win a battle against not just one foe but many; The heads of the hydra. Health issues, financial issues, social benefits (the double minded one), lack of time, lack of skill and resources, supporting family (the trial we actually appreciate).

It's a dangerous thing, this stopping; breathing and looking at things in a different way...Things are never quite what they seem. A New and Brighter View has come to mind.

Other than budgeting and time table planning, whether you are trying to get off benefits or not as I mentioned in the previous chapter, build a food storage and learn how to use it (i.e. learn about appropriate prepping).Get out and stay out of debt and avoid buying anything unless it is necessary and then only if you have saved for it first. General good sense really. Build up at least 2 months' worth credit in the bank to cover the bills while upheavals are worked out. Cash if you are on benefits and it could take a year to build up that kind of reserve.

Another handy tool, if you don't already have an immaculate and perfectly ordered life, do a bunch of clearing out. For one, it will feel good and remove clutter which just adds stress. For two, you might come across items you no longer need and can sell. Stick that in the penny jar. Call the jar your freedom bank. *Seriously! Why can't we add emoji icons in books?!?*

I know I'm repeating myself here but just as a recap and because when something is important, it's worth repeating.

Living this way can be tricky because it means you go through the same difficulty in forming new habits but at the same time, it's easier and quicker to form new habits than it is to quit old ones.

It takes months to build that kind of reserve, sometimes years, especially if you are on social welfare. I know. That's why it's taken years to get this far for us. In that sense, your future survival depends on the preparations and mindset you make and live with NOW.

I will cover this a bit more in another book specifically.

11

ABUNDANT MINDSET STUFF
A NEW AND BRIGHTER VIEW

"Because needs must and there IS a better way"

That's been a motivation for me for many years. In one way when you first read it, it sounds like one of those 'grass is greener on the other side' statements. You know? When you're never satisfied with what you have and looking for something better.

That's not where I'm coming from. I'm coming from a point where maybe something isn't good, it's either wrong or isn't functioning the way it should.

That's when we'll find a better way because 'needs must'. There IS a better way, because obviously there is more than one way to do something and maybe it just needs a NEW way of doing or looking at things.

For instance; instead of continuing to use only tap water to water our plants, increasing the amount of treated water in the garden and putting extra strain on the water treatment plants, water supply companies (and environmental/social consideration), we can harvest the rainwater that would otherwise keep our garden a muddy bog or which would merely run off the roofs into the guttering and down the drain. Harvesting or catching and storing rainwater then deliberately using and directing whathappens to it, we're using healthier water for the plants, and being less extractive and more regenerative for nature. Oh, and paying lessout on water bills.

By properly fitting overflow pipes to the water butts, we can avoid the water logging of the garden and lead excess to the drains (if in the countryside with more land, I could store the water on the land and allow overflow into a stream or river if there is NOWHERE left in the land for it to go). In the suburbs there's only so much you can store and use, especially in Ireland or Wales where traditionally (not so much now) the rainfall has always been what they are known for because of the mountains.

I hope you get what I'm saying. It's not a complaint to look for a better way. It's about making the most of what we have and increasing its value to us and nature, or our finances, our health, our self-reliance and self-sufficiency.

That positive mindset of gratitude is part of what led to the times I stopped and took stock, counted blessings and then had the Lightbulb moments.

Some came like the dimmer switch brightening and others like a slap in the face. All of them, leading us along the path to our dream in very different ways than we might have liked or planned. Foundations and dreaming are part of the journey.

Two of my favourite quotes;

"Purposes, like eggs, unless they are hatched into action, will run into decay". (Samuel Smiles) and

"If you have ambitions, dream of what you wish to accomplish and then put your shoulder to the wheel and work. Daydreams without work do not amount to anything; it is the actual work that counts". (Heber J. Grant)

That's exactly what we've always tried to do...put our shoulders to the wheel and work.

I've mentioned before I'm sure, I don't believe in consequences. If not, now you know. I feel there are purposes in and a plan for everything. People usually want evidence of it but it's everywhere and in everything. Nature proves it with its patterns and variety. It's designed. Everything has a purpose.

So for me to stop, take stock, evaluate past, present and hoped for future, that stocktake has to include the hydra. If there is a purpose and reason for everything, what's the purpose or reason for the hydra in our lives?

If the desire, need and drive for the direction we have been going in feels like we were pointed in that direction, why the opposition?

Didn't I already mention that in 2019, I realised we DID actually have the dream (even if not quite as planned)? There was definitely as I explained a load of opposition and yet, here we are.

We have the 'land' complete with an orchard and veggie garden. We have the 'cottage' complete with cottage garden and veranda. We grow, preserve and store what we have, sharing the excess. We make a home, craft and try to live greenly. We are also trying to make our homestead part of our financial self-reliance.

It almost feels like during the realization of the dream, we were like children being coaxed, urged and commanded to cross a bridge we didn't know was a way out by someone who had our backs and was our guardian, directing us in a way that would get us over those bridges in spite of the hydra. .

Reminds me, I don't know about you, but I really love the Nanny McPhee movies. The book isn't as epic as the movies to me. It's usually the other way around. The imagery and the story line really struck a chord with me. As you already might know, this nanny was uninvited and hideous to look at (at first, to the children). They thought of her as yet another bully determined to force obedience. They weren't having it and were going to get rid of her the same way they got rid of all the others.

Well, as you also already might know, she was way too smart and experienced for them and had this kind of power about her. She reminded me of yet another famous Victorian nanny (*Look, I don't want any copyright trouble coming my way. You know which nannies I mean*) with her ability to convince others that her ideas were theirs in the first place.That power used to be called feminine wiles but is way more than that. I call it bringing the best out of people. In fact, it's what I call grandma magic.It's the power of love, wisdom, compassion, insight, understanding, knowledge coupled with feminine spirit.

Anyway, these nannies helped the children (and the parents), take responsibility for their choices with firm but loving guidance. The children realised as they went along and got to know them better, things weren't what they seemed. They saw them differently. The families grew to love them and they were closer than ever. The families wanted them to stay...but of course, that's not how they work. I'm nowhere near that 'magical' but I aspire to inspire love, compassion, responsibility, courage, self-reliance and resilience in those around me. I'll let you know when I've cracked it. It may take some time.

As I have done a number of times now, I repeat the important stuff. It brings back the quote from Don Campbell. Just in case you've forgotten, "If you want to make minor changes, change the way you DO things. If you want to make major changes, change the way you SEE things".

If things are repeated, it's because they are so important. You already know where I'm going with this, don't you...Or maybe not.

I have taught myself to see a different side or possibility to all trials and in particular, our whole situation. Unlike the mythological Sirens misleading the sailors to their deaths, our hydra has never pretended to be anything but a man made beast, blocking our progress, stealing our dreams, freedoms and being at least a frustration.

96

In reality, it's just one of those parts of life and like all trials, experiences and so on;we can learn, move forward and grow from them.

Most of our trials are the natural consequences of being in a mortal realm with its limits on lifespan and resultant weaknesses and illnesses or natural disasters. Some consequences are the results of either our own choices and actions and some the consequences of other peoples' choices and actions. Like politicians and their agendas.

Maybe if I'd chosen to see things differently earlier, we would have arrived here quicker...Now that's in the realms of "could've, should've, would've".

No point going there. But it makes you think, doesn't it? Nothing is quite as it seems and if everything has a purpose and reason and there are no such thing as coincidence, just maybe there's a kinder, more caring and guiding hand we aren't even aware of.

No matter what trials we ever go through, how we come out the other end of them could entirely depend on the way we choose to see them.

I don't mean putting on those 'rose tinted glasses', but do mean, to have an element of Pollyanna's Glad Game. Recognise the horrible side of it, the reality of its effects, then also find a silver lining, something to be glad about.

Sometimes, 'the lessons hardest learned are the ones least forgotten'. I can't tell you where that one came from. What we work hardest for and struggle with, we treasure more, and we wouldn't know what sweet is if we've never tasted bitter.

If every trial is a preparation to kit us with the tools to be able to tackle the next, then if we remember to adjust our perspective spectacles we will be able to weather the coming storms in our lives or even the global or national prospect of financial depression, whether globally or personally. So far there's over 32 thousand words in this book so I can't remember if I have mentioned before, that it's out of difficult times and situations that some of the greatest inventions and ideas have arisen.

Writing this book has been a stock take and reflection in itself. I feel a contradiction in my mind,afraid but calm and excited all at the same time. I feel hopeful and satisfied that we have actually got this far so we can make it further.

Writing has helped me to do one massive Stock take of blessings. It has taken me down memory lane in a good way and opened my mind to see so much more than what's on the surface.

Before I leave you with my parting thoughts, I have a sort of confession to make.

All through this book, I have stated that my husband and self have had the same dream. We have, 'The Good Life'. We both want land, Self-sufficiency, self-reliance and connection with nature and greater relationships with people. There's a difference though in our perspectives.

It's what I said before about the way we see things. Even though my eyes have been opened to see that we already have elements of that dream, hestill wants that good life abroad. So what do I do about that? Try to force him to see things my way?

Why the heck would I do that to the man who has always, over more than 34 years, gone along with MY ideas and supported me in everything I do even when it wasn't what he wanted and even at times at the cost of his comfort and peace of mind?

He has always been supportive of everything I do. Now what I am about to say might look like a contradiction or weird. Hear me out.

I have come to the realisation that my own version of our dream has come true. I am doing all I set out to do and even though only in the beginning stages of my writing dream, I have for all intents and purposes arrived. I'd call it an even greater success when we are completely self-reliant and have a positive bank balance.

My dream now includes making HIS dream a reality. I have learned over the 34+ years that we achieve more and quicker when we are 'equally yoked' and progressing side by side instead of dashing ahead like a bull in a china shop. So how did I know that and still we aren't quite on the same page?

That's because his foundations were not the same as mine and his perspective spectacles are a different hue. To be honest he has said that if land and property weren't so stupidly expensive here in the UK and we could afford a smallholding further south, He would jump at it.

I intend to make a fortune to buy his dream, because that's what it will take. I will happily evolve MY dream to OURS. I won't be giving mine up. Everything I have learned and discovered will continue with me and us. My new goal is to make our dreams one. Hopefully, affording it he will have changed his mind about the abroad thing.

My home and heart is with him. Blue Garden Cottage is the same wherever it ends up. It's not a place. I have done it before and I will do it again if I have to.

Now, I want to explore 'Abundance Mindset' a bit more with you. It might just help you change the way YOU see things and the direction you need or want to go in your own path. It might just help you find the best way for you to make the most of your life and situation or find solutions and improve your self-reliance. For some folk just being able to get a job that pays and gaining their freedom from the dole IS the dream.

I have already spoken about scarcity and abundance mindsets. Maybe you already know all this. In which case I suggest that there are so many different ways of coming to the same outcome and I hope then just to add to the pool of information already out there.

Another disclaimer as a reminder; I am neither a psychologist nor a life coach. I have no such qualifications. What I share is NOT advice or instruction. I am simply offering more information to

you that I have learned from others and from my own experiences which I feel is of value to me and I hope it might be to you too. What I'm sharing is freely available all over the internet and I have always believed that just because it's on the internet does NOT make it fact or truth. Instead, treat it as a tool to sift out what applies to you and see if it works.

We're back to mindset now. I think you can tell all the way through this book that I believe in going with your gut. I also am a Christian and therefore have a grasp for and belief that we are all spiritual beings having a mortal experience. I therefore feel there's more to life than the everyday grind for the temporal things we feel we HAVE to have, get or do.

That comes with an understanding that we are here for a purpose and with a responsibility as stewards of all that we 'have'. I also believe that a part of our purpose is to find joy in the experience even surrounded by all those consequences of mortality I've been talking about all the way through.

Everyone has their own beliefs and understandings which I find wonderful. To have such variety in the world is truly amazing. I try to sift out the good or rather the things that uplift, inspire and feed and encourage the human soul elevating them to their best. I love learning from people of all understandings and opinions.

It would be great if we all respected each others' opinions without feeling the need to correct or put down someone's knowledge because it doesn't fit with our own. Just because someone might not agree with our ideas and doesn't take it on board, doesn't mean we or they are wrong. I value our gift to choose for ourselves and would benefit from respecting others' right and gift to do the same.

That said, it doesn't mean I don't disagree with others on some topics. I think we can be different and disagree without contention or hard feelings, and still show love compassion and kindness.

And so, every word in this book is based on my own opinion, beliefs, experience and understanding. Take what you will or nothing. I respect your choice. I'm just very grateful for you even buying this book as it helps me on that journey to self-reliance and financial freedom. So thank you from the bottom of my heart.

Ok, that's enough squidgy talk!, back to the abundant mindset stuff. From my months of study into the subject and listening to a whole bunch of podcasts, then doing my pondering and evaluation thing, I have found that many of the things spoken about, I already knew and learned from my study of scripture and other religious discourses or talks. I have also learned much from the essays of C. S. Lewis in his book, Mere Christianity. I really love that one.

The most basic start to increasing your wealth, health and happiness begins with an attitude of gratitude. It is the simplest thing we can do even if not easiest but quickest way to start a massive change in our lives. I have already spoken about Pollyanna's Glad Game from the movie and mentioned a number of quotes reinforcing that idea.

I have always felt that if you have never experienced even a small bit of discomfort or trials, you wouldn't be able to recognise or appreciate the good or wonderful side as everything in existence has an opposite. How can you compare and know what it is without something to compare it with?

So when I drink a glass of cold tap water on a very hot day after working physically in the garden, as I sip the water I sigh and thank God for water, for indoor plumbing, for creation and something to drink the water from.There is nothing so beautiful as a glass of water to quench thirst in that moment.

Being grateful adds value to whatever we are grateful for and connects us with the reality that we are connected with things, people and dependent on each other so we never get arrogant and prideful or complacent which are the opposite of abundant thinking.

The more we show and demonstrate gratitude, the more abundant we feel. We recognise what we do have instead of what we don't. We can share more too and lift others to more abundant thinking too. That way, our environments are more pleasant. Feelings ripple out and do affect everyone and everything around us. I mentioned the smile being as contagious as a cold before.

How many times have you been in the company of someone angry, cynical, contentious and rude and come away feeling good? I bet never or rarely. Being moody casts a shadow around us and makes us less attractive to be around and I don't mean in appearance I mean our personality and the atmosphere around us. I can tell you now, that when I'm in a bad mood, my family very quickly sense it and the bad mood spreads, things just seem to go wrong all the way through the day, unless I stop and reset. Gratitude is a great reset button.

The opposite of abundance is the negative traits of dishonesty, negativity, cynicism, complaining, cheating, lying, greed, treating others unkindly, selfishness, cruelty and abuse of any kind. Critical judgment, hating or being jealous of others' wealth or health, envy,these traits are not the ones that would attract any kind of good or positive people, things or even wealth to you. Nobody wants to be around such traits nor are people inclined to share with those types of traits. I want to stress that these are not what people ARE but what we DO. Every action or thought has a consequence.

Abundant mindset traits include all the positive attributes you would imagine, likehonesty, integrity, positivity, gratitude, generosity, kindness, forgiveness, respect, transparency, using discernment to judge situations and people or things in a good way. It's allowing ourselves to be happy for others in their good situations instead of being jealous or wanting their life (covetousness), but genuinely rejoicing in wellbeing (yours or others'). These traits attract people and things TO you.

Of course we are not perfect and all have our off days when we are not our best. Like I said, we can't know the sweet without the bitter,either in ourselves or seeing them in others to compare. Thankfully we CAN choose how we respond. We can choose our thoughts, attitudes and actions. We can correct ourselves with kindness and forgiveness. We can redirect ourselves.

It's ok to make mistakes and have off days and then move on from them. Our past doesn't define who or what we are but how we use it can form our characters and determine what sort of energy, people or environment we attract to ourselves. That includes our self-reliance journeys.

Changing 'I will in the future' and 'one day' statements in our minds and then our speech to'right now' and 'I am' statements, living our lives now as if we already were the people we want to be or are already in the jobs we want to have, or are in the relationships we want to have, will put us in the frame of mind to become and have those things.

For instance, if I want to be in a specific job, I would do the things I would do if I already had that job. In my daily routine, I would get up and get dressed accordingly, prepare my day for work and then set to work on something, preferably whatever will increase my chances of getting that job. I would dress appropriately for that job even if I don't yet have it. I would fill my time studying what is needed for that job and gain whatever I need.

I've referred to my video of I'm the Boss of Me. I still can choose if I actually do anything or not and I am ultimately the one who has to get myself out of bed and do what needs to be done or what I want to do. I can change that 'need to do' to an 'I want to do' statement.

I can get out of bed in the morning feeling groggy and not wanting to get up complaining or I can get up with a thankful heart, be grateful for another day and make the most of it. It also helps if you go to bed at the right time and in the right frame of mind to influence the morning. There's a lot more to it than that but it's good enough to make my point.

OK, you get it.

So then, in my own self-reliance, dreaming, life changing, dole escaping endeavours, here are some of the thoughts, phrases, sayings, scriptures and whatever that I have found most helpful and guiding to me. Even though I realised I have been studying and learning these things for years I am only now beginning to implement them more deliberately. If you implement any of these, you and I will be on the same journey of onward and upwards.

We're going to get rid of lies and misleading statements like; 'there's never enough money', 'only the lucky and the rich make money', 'I can't afford it', 'money comes one hand and immediately out the other', 'money is gone before it even comes in'. **Ban** anything like it from our conversations and our language with ourselves, our children and family. We aren't putting blinkers on. We are changing the way money is attracted to us, how we use it and view it. We are changing our habits and lifestyles to make it easier for money to come to us.

We are going to get rid of the idea that 'money is the root of all evil'. I'll tell you why. The statement in fact is a misreading of a verse in 1 Timothy, Chapter 6, verse10 in the New Testament of the Christian Bible. It states; '...for the LOVE of money is the root of all evil'. It's the LOVE of it and selfish, greedy, corrupt use of it. THAT more accurately is what the scripture teaches. Instead, love the good you can do WITH money. There's no need to put ourselves on a guilt trip if we have money. So we are going to question every negative thing we feel, have learned or hear about money.

We are going to dismiss ideas that we are too old for certain jobs, too old to change, too set in our ways, 'that's just the way it is', 'that's just the way I am'.

Instead we are going to start helpful and positive statements with 'I AM' … perfectly employable (if a job is what we want), healthy, young, fit. 'I AM a magnet for money and it comes to me easily, in increasing amounts by various means'. And we are going to tell ourselves that in the mirror, out loud, every day until we believe it and it becomes real. Until we behave in the way we would if we were already in that state. 'I AM' statements take us away from the past and bring our future intentions into the now. After all, 'Tomorrow will always be tomorrow. It never arrives'. Today is always here and now.

We begin our day and end it with gratitude for at least 5 things. I bet we can come up with way more than that. Let it be our first and last thoughts every day, because 'what you give is what you get'.

We are going to get up and get dressed ready for the day and tell ourselves that we are amazing beings with the capacity to change our worlds and lives.

We are eternal being occupying a mortal body to help us navigate this mortal world AND experience joy in it. So we are going to tell our bodies that we are grateful for them doing what they do to keep us going and we will commit to treating them better so that they can help us enjoy all that our bodies can help us experience.

We are going to breathe deeply and MOVE,in whatever way we can. Call it exercise or just a stroll; go for a run if able. Dance, wiggle that bum in our chair but MOVE!

We eat as wholesomely as we can,educate ourselves on whole foods nutrition and move away from processed stuff. We make choices that will help us to get the foods needed to help our bodies function at their best, because 'What you put in is what you get out' and because we are worth the effort.

'If you do today what you did yesterday, what you got yesterday is all you will get today'.

'People tend to move in the direction they are looking so look and choose where you are going'.

105

People will only see in us what we see in ourselves.

Let that same pattern be the way we handle all the aspects of our lives and I am convinced that we will see results and be stunned at the progress made in our journeys.

I can't believe it has taken me so long to grasp these principles when I have had them all along!

So I'm going to go back to my original questions.

Do you still have a dream?

What has been the driving force in your life and what are your foundations?

What obstacles have got in the way of your dream realization and what's your WHY?

Have you got a plan?

Are you now where you thought you would be when you first dreamed?

I really hope that in sharing our own journey with you that you might have been moved forward in YOUR dreams or even in daring to dream at all.

I hope that you will be able to find a new and brighter view for the future in spite of and despite current global, national or personal situations. I hope that you too will be able to adjust your own perspective spectacles to see clearly a route out of your situation and into a clearer path.

Our journey in Blue Garden Cottage is just at the beginning. It's constantly changing and evolving every day. It's my goal to report back to you soon in achieving self-reliance completely.

Yesterday I would have said, 'Who knows where we will be in a year's time'. Now I say, 'I am an author and I am self-reliant'. What a massive adventure! Here's wishing you a wonderful adventure too.

The only thing left for me to share with you is a list of all my favourite books, YouTube channels, websites and magazines.

I'm leaving you with love, hope and a new friend.
Seriously, that is The End... of this book.

MY FAVOURITE RECOURCES

I have found so many helpful channels, books and a couple of magazines over the years. All helpful or interesting but my favourites are the only ones I am going to share with you. Even in my book cases, there are loads of books I use but only the most relevant ones are listed. Some channels I repeat because they cover a few different topics. It just seemed easier to list them all in topics

YouTube Channels
No-Dig Gardening:
- Charles Dowding
- Liz Zorab - Byther Farm
- My Family Garden
- Forest Gardening:
- Martin Crawford
- Robert Heart
- Bealtaine Cottage
- Liz Zorab - Byther Farm

Permaculture:
- Patric Whitefield
- Bill Mollison
- Geoff Lawton: Permaculture Online
- David Holmgren
- Bealtaine Cottage
- Liz Zorab - Byther Farm

Natural and Green Living:
- Fairyland Cottage
- Girl in Calico
- Bealtaine Cottage
- Pick Up Lymes
- SustainabilityIllustrated.

Homesteading and Frugal Living:
- Suburban Homestead (Siloe Oliveira)
- Rain Country
- Bealtaine Cottage
- Coffee With Kate
- Fairyland Cottage
- Elliot Homestead

111

- What Vivi Did Next

Health and Wellbeing:
- Pick Up Lymes
- Fairyland Cottage
- Taiflow
- Yoga with Adriene

Writing and Course Creation:
- Gillian Perkins (Author and Self-Publishing and online business instructor)

Heart Breathings (Sara Cannon - author and Self-publishing instructor)

•

BOOKS

These are in no particular order of importance either, just favourites in category.

Gardening and Homesteading:
- Small gardens - David Stevens
- The Cottage Garden - Polly Bolton
- The Practical Book of Self-Sufficiency - John Seymore
- How to Grow Winter Veg - Charles Dowding
- Permaculture in a Nutshell - Patrick Whitefield
- How to Grow Perennial Veg - Martin Crawford
- Plants for a Future - Ken Fern
- The New Complete Book of Self-Sufficiency - John Seymore
- The Cottage Garden Diaries - Fiona J. Houston

- Home Storage and Production for the British Isles -Pauline Dogget Smith (this one might be out of print and at the time of writing this, there were only 3 on Amazon and were over £30 so very expensive for a small paperback. It looks like it's a collectible because one reads 'very rare copy'. Mine is one of those rare copies.)

Natural and Green living:
- Pure Living - How to Detox Your Home - Sally Bevan
- Organic Living - Michael Van Straten
- Prepping:

- Living off Nature - Judy Urquhart
- Food for Free - Richard Mabey
- The Homesteader's Herbal Companion - Amy Fewel
- Jekka's Complete Herb Book - Jekka McVicar
- Grow Your Own Drugs - James Wong
- Home Storage and Production for the British Isles Pauline Dogget Smith
- Feeding the Nation - Marguerite Patten OBE

Wellbeing:
- The Encyclopaedia of Essential Oils - Julia Lawless
- New Vital Oils - Liz Earle
- The Big Bean Cookbook - Nicola Graimes
- Forks Over Knives - AlonaPulde - MD and Matthew Lederman – MD
- The Herb and Flower Cookbook - Pip McCormac
- Mere Christianity - C S Lewis

Writing and Course Creation:
- Passion to Profit - Andy Harrington
- Ultimate Course Formula - Iman Aghay

Magazines
- Permaculture Magazine -Permanent Publications
- Country Living (obviously UK)
- Turn Your Hobby into a Business - by Country Living
- The Big Book of Crafting by Period Living

Of course above all these resources, by far the best and my favorite books are my scriptures. They're the most read of all my books and have had a greater effect on my life than all the above put together. That's another foundation stone.

ACKNOWLEDGEMENTS

There have literally been thousands of people who have throughout my life contributed their knowledge, personal experiences and skills to me,so I thank them all.

The most important and influential people though are first, my Heavenly Father who has given me all and had a hand in my life from day one;

Then my husband who has always stepped back to let me do my thing and watched me fly, coming along for the ride no matter how inconvenient or annoying. He too has brought me so much love and joy;

Then there's my children and grandchildren who have been a part of my journey learning about myself as far as developing patience, endurance and most of all, for making my heart swell with love and joy;

My parents who against all odds and without a manual actually managed to raise someone who isn't all together nuts, who did the best they could to teach me to survive and thrive with what knowledge they had/have.

My dad for sharing his artistic talents with me, my mum for her amazing make do and mend, homemaking, frugal skills that have been the biggest influence in giving me skills to ensure my family never went hungry, cold or neglected.

I'd also like to acknowledge my best friend Chris, who encourages and supports me in everything I do and shares so many of my hobbies and passions as far as style, crafts and nature go.

Everything I do and am is a culmination of generations of people, their influence and experiences which have all come together to help me recognize where I am in the evolution of Blue Garden Cottage.

ABOUT THE AUTHOR

Sindy Wakeham is a writer and book creator living in Wales. She is a suburban homesteader turning her suburban council house home into the dream homesteading cottage and gardens she always wanted. Not even financial struggles would get in the way. She does that by using frugal and Permaculture principles in her home and garden. Nature, crafting, homemaking, gardening and above those, her family and faith are her inspiration. The goal is to gain self-reliance for her family and herself by writing and creating her own business and inspiring others to reach for and build their choice of life no matter the obstacles.

You can learn more about Sindy and Blue Garden Cottage at
https://www.youtube.com/@BlueGardenCottage .

Printed by BoD™in Norderstedt, Germany